BUILDING TRUST

The First Step to Successful Project Management

A. Jamshed Adel

PM-Panacea

Building Trust: The First Step to Successful Project Management

Copyright ©2020 by PM-Panacea, LLC

Acknowledgements

Writing this book would have been impossible without the support, advice, motivation, and encouragement of my beautiful wife, Sosan Shariq Adel. From the time I met Sosan, she has been behind every single success in my life. I am deeply thankful and indebted to her for being an exceptional spouse, partner, friend, listener, supporter, motivator, advisor, and many more! Without you, I would not be the person I am today.

I would also like to thank my beautiful daughter, Armaghan Adel, who pleasantly sacrificed her *daddy-daughter* time for a long time so I can write my book. Thank you Armie, and I hope I can make it up for you!

Finally, I would like to thank my wonderful mom for being a great mother, my first teacher, and striving to provide me with every opportunity to learn as a kid during the most difficult times. Thank you for everything, Mom!

Contents

Foreword

In today's digital landscape and global economy, global corporations erase boundaries and merge cultures. Multinational corporations hire employees from around the globe, increasing the complexity of corporate culture and climate, and the challenge facing organizations is finding common ground beyond the rising incivility among individuals. As these corporations continue to hire employees from around the world, individual cultures merge with organizational ones. Each semester, I welcome a diverse group of students to my digital classroom with many objectives and one overarching goal: for each individual to gain more than just textbook knowledge.

As an educator, I believe that respect for my students is essential in earning their trust, and that trust, once earned, is the pathway to developing a deeper, more meaningful atmosphere for learning. Every consequential interaction is based on trust – and free of the Machiavellian idea of fear. As a scholar-practitioner, I believe communication is a critical component of success for project managers, but without trust, what is being communicated loses volume in the conversation. This is why A. Jamshed Adel's book resonated with me. Trust is a vital component for managing projects to success. Why? Because individuals share knowledge with those they perceive as trustworthy. Lauded leaders trust their teams to get the job done. Individuals who trust their teams and their leaders aren't afraid to contribute to the conversation.

In his book, Jamshed provides an overview of the concept of trust and demonstrates why trust is a key ingredient in project management. He shares his created concept for how to execute projects successfully leveraging the EMPOWER framework through trust. Since lack of trust is reported as a key barrier to knowledge sharing, Jamshed's book provides a cautionary look at how projects fail when trust is not built among the team members and knowledge is never shared. By examining trust along-side the key components of project management, *Building Trust: The First Step to Successful Project Management* demonstrates how trust integrates with project success.

Simon Cleveland, Ph.D.
Faculty Director
Georgetown University

Introduction

If you are in the world of technology, you may not be surprised to read that the success rate of technology projects is barely at 30%—yes, despite being in the era of modern technology! According to one report, only 29% of over 25,000 technology projects from 2011 to 2015 have been successful (Standish Group International, Inc., 2015). Most of the projects are completed over budget, late, under-delivered, or they completely fail. This is an alarming number! Why do so few projects succeed? What factors contribute to the project challenges and failures? Poor scope definition, lack of user involvement, poorly defined requirements, inadequate resources, poor project management, and poor testing are among some of the key factors that lead projects to challenges and failures (Mwanza & Namusokwe, 2015). These factors can be rolled up into four major categories: poor planning, poor execution, poor quality control, and poor communication.

Multiple research studies suggest that many projects failed and/or faced challenges (with budget, scope, quality, and time) because they had planning issues (Mwanza & Namusokwe, 2015; Stepanek, 2005; Imudia, Kaindaneh, & Baffour-Awuah, 2013; Malone, n.d.; Shauchenka, n.d.). Whether you are planning for sprints/iterations, project phases, or the entire project, planning remains a prerequisite for successful project delivery. Regardless of the type of project or project management methodology, before moving into the execution phase of your project, at a minimum you need to define your project goals and objectives, your project stakeholders, users' needs, deliverables and activities (and/or phases and sprints), required skills and capabilities, quality requirements, project budget, communication strategies, risks, assumptions, and constraints. Planning, on the other hand, does not mean that you must produce a 100-page plan document for your project. I am talking about effective planning that may differ from one project to another in terms of depth and scale, depending on applicable project factors and circumstances. As a project manager and leader, it is important that you determine what effective planning for your project means.

The next major failure aspect of projects is poor execution. The way a project plan is implemented, how the project team is acquired and led, and the methods through which a project works, stakeholders, quality, risks, time, cost, change, and many other elements of how a project is managed determines the success levels of each project. Many of the success factors such as "emotional maturity, ...user involvement, ...optimization, ...skilled resources, ...[and] modest execution" listed in the Chaos Report by Standish Group International, Inc. (2015) indicate that poor execution has played a key role in challenging and leading technology projects to failures. No matter how impeccable a project plan is, it is the *execution* that counts at the end of the day.

Poor quality does not only guarantee project failure but can also cost lives and leave a long-lasting catastrophic impact. An example of poor quality control can be seen in the Firestone Wilderness AT tires that caused a significant number of deaths and injuries due to treads detaching from tires at high speeds (leading to loss of vehicle control) in the 1990s and was finally recalled by the manufacturer in August 2000 (U.S. Department of Transportation, 2001). This fatal defect could have been prevented had there been appropriate quality control measures in place.

The minimum impact of poor testing and quality control is a waste of time and money (besides reputation and loss of credibility). I remember a few years ago when our project faced major reworks due to poor testing that was only performed on a small component of the system. This resulted in several weeks of delays and additional costs. Quality control is the third, but a key determining factor, of success in projects.

What do you think high performing project managers do most of the time? They communicate. According to Project Management Institute, project managers spend 90% of their time communicating (Project Management Institute, 2017). They communicate with their project team, project sponsors/senior management, users and clients, partners, and many other groups of stakeholders. In fact, the only way I differentiate between a good project manager and an excellent project manager is by how often and effectively they communicate. Effective communication is the fourth but most important element that sets the project stage for conquest.

How can we ensure successful project planning, execution, quality control, and communication? For many years in the early stages of my project management career, I was asking the same question. After years of curiosity, research, and assessment of my own track record, I found one fundamental answer that I call the *project management panacea*. And that is *TRUST*. When trust is present across the project, you can build realistic project plans, ensure successful execution and quality control, and build and maintain transparent and effective channels of communication among project stakeholders. By doing so, you will be able to increase the odds of winning not only in your projects, but with your project management and leadership career as well. In fact, trust is the cornerstone, the mainstay, and the fuel for successful project management. This is the very reason that has inspired me to write this book.

This book is divided in two major parts. The first part discusses the importance of trust in project planning, execution, quality control, and communication. The second part provides you with a framework to build trust with your seniors, project teams, and stakeholders. By the end of this book, you will be able to draw some actionable strategies to use trust as a key tool in managing and leading your projects.

Part One

The Role of Trust in Projects

What does trust mean? Before we discuss the influence of trust in projects, it is important to understand what trust means in this context. Merriam-Webster provides several definitions for trust; however, we will refer to the following definitions.

> Trust (as a noun): "assured reliance on the character, ability, strength, or truth of someone..." (Merriam-Webster, 2020)

> Trust (as a verb): "to place confidence in: rely on [someone]" (Merriam-Webster, 2020)

Whether you are a project coordinator, manager, or leader, trust must be at the core of your behavior. Projects are about getting from point A to point B. Trust is the fuel that enables the project team to continue moving toward point B. Without this integral fuel, you can hardly get to your target. Lack of trust creates negative politics, doubt, reluctance, low interest and motivation, lack of commitment, unhappiness, negative conflict, finger-pointing, and many other destructions among your team that will ultimately push your project off the cliff.

When these trust issues emerge, everyone in the project switches to either the plaintiff or defendant mode. No one will take responsibility for their actions and admit their mistakes. No one will be transparent. Everyone will have hidden agendas. The focus will not be on the project anymore—it will be focused on selves. The primary goal will switch to surviving and saving jobs and paychecks. As a project manager, you will spend most of your time dealing with these problems. You will have to verify and re-verify every piece of information you receive from your team. You will be blamed by senior management, sponsors, clients, and other relevant stakeholders for not making any progress. You will be forced to take the defendant mode. You will end up hiding issues from people at the top of the chain, and deal with your project issues without any necessary executive sponsorship support. You will focus on polishing project reports and showing green lights in every part of your project. These are just some of the many consequences for simply lacking one element in your team—*trust*. Trust is the remedy for every challenge in your project.

Trust ensures you have a realistic plan for your project. It creates transparency, reliability, and a culture of commitment and responsibility within your team. It will help you identify and prevent problems and will assist to continuously improve during project execution. It will also ensure reliable quality control by your team. Finally, trust will help you and your team communicate effectively and transparently. No one will have hidden agendas anymore. Everything will be discernable and on the surface. And one more thing: while trust is contagious, distrust is twice as contagious. Trust me!

Chapter One

Trust and Project Planning

As you might agree, project planning is not a one-time deliverable. It is continuous. Whether you are applying predictive (traditional/waterfall), iterative (agile), or a blended project management approach, you constantly assess and adapt your plan to ensure efficacy and relevance as you move through your project's lifecycle (unless your project plan has been locked for any changes, which in itself creates trust issues within the team). When planning for any type of project, at a minimum, your goal is to find answers to the following questions:

1. Why does the project exist? What are the needs of the users?
2. What needs to be done (in terms of creating product or service) to meet the needs of the users?
3. What do the pieces/segments of the product or service look like?
4. What work will be involved to make each piece/segment of the product or service?
5. What skills, capabilities, and tools do we need to complete the work?
6. How are we going to acquire and manage the skills, capabilities, and tools?

7. In what order do we need to do the work? How long do we need for each piece of work?

8. What is the definition of completed work?

9. How can we ensure quality; prevent, and/or manage work defects and issues?

10. How should the pieces/segments be put together?

11. What are the issues, threats, and opportunities? How are we going to manage these elements?

12. Who has a stake and/or influence in the project? How are we going to manage their expectations? How are we going to communicate effectively with them?

Answers to these questions make up your project plan and performance baselines. Unless you are a one-man army completing a project in a desert, to get answers to your questions you need to depend on a number of project stakeholders, including users, clients, project sponsors/senior management, the project team, functional managers, partners, suppliers, subcontractors, etc. The more transparent and honest the answers, the more realistic and effective your project plan will be, and the richer your goals and targets will be. Here is the one-million-dollar question (or one billion if you are a millionaire!): How do you make sure you get the answers that you are expecting, and how do you minimize *diplomatic* answers to your questions? There may be, and there are, many considerations that will help you achieve this goal. However, I guarantee that in the absence of *trust* within your network, you will not be able to get honest, transparent, reliable answers. And when I say trust, I refer to that of mutual trust. You trust them and they trust you.

However, as the leading player in your project, your first step should be to cultivate the seed. How? The second part of this book will give you in-depth answers to this question. For now, let us dive deeper in our discussion on the importance of this paramount phenomenon, trust, in project planning.

Project Definition

You might concur with me that the project definition, which you may also refer to as the project charter, project initiation, or project authorization document, is key to project planning. In fact, all the components of the project plan will be built upon this document, so it is particularly important that the information provided in the document is valid. At this point, you might whisper, "Well, it is not the project manager and the project team who defines the project. The project definition is passed down by management and we are told by them to make it happen within the given constraints." This is true, and in most cases, this is what happens. So, do not worry, you are not alone on this ship. But have you ever wondered why this happens?

I asked the same question to one of the executive members of a company I was working with. At that time, he was a great friend of mine. I asked him what his thoughts were around pushing down targets and decisions for projects without involving the project managers and why this happens. He gave me a short and sweet answer, "We don't trust them." His answers to my follow up questions revealed that it wasn't that he (and his executive colleagues) didn't think that the project managers were incapable.

It was more about hidden agendas and personal interests. In other words, the project managers had not proven that they shared the same interests, goals, and vision with their senior team. I told him frankly (I knew he was not going to fire an honest friend) that it is them as the leaders who must build trust; that they should stop the culture of pointing fingers and blaming, and instead nourish an environment of shared responsibility. That is how they create reliable project managers who can take pieces of the burden when it comes to the project decisions.

If your senior management does not initiate the first step of planting the first seed, then you should. And do not forget to water the plant of trust so you can harvest what you expect. Trust between you, senior leadership, clients, and the project team ensures that you work together to define the project goals, objectives, and scope in the most pragmatic way possible.

Time and Cost Estimates

As discussed above, time and cost estimates are usually constrained in the project definition document. This will cause the project manager and team to estimate cost and time backward (top-down). To verify (or reverify) the feasibility of achieving the project scope within the given time and cost limitations, it is important for estimates to come from the project team and subject matter experts (bottom-up estimation).

However, I have rarely seen this scenario materialize because of the lack of trust between management and the project team. As a result, the project manager and team must make adjustments (or compromises) to match the lower level timelines and costs with the imposed budget and schedule end targets.

Furthermore, in the worst-case scenario, the first group who will not buy into the cost and schedule baselines is the project team itself. The baseline becomes baseless right from the start! As a result, for the rest of the project, the project manager and team will struggle to keep up with the target. Trust will deteriorate more and more every day. On the other hand, what if senior management has confidence in the project team? What if the project team trusts the management? When there is trust, there is more listening, collaboration, and transparency. Every side will work hard to make realistic cost and time estimates;

and if they do not know, they will admit it and ask for help rather than providing fabricated answers. This leads to building a project plan on healthy, strong baselines.

Risk Management

One important aspect of project planning is the identification of opportunities (positive risks) and threats (negative risks) that could potentially impact the project. Every single team member and project stakeholder plays an equally vital role in maximizing opportunities and minimizing threats. With lack of trust, there will be less motivation for the team to contribute to the identification of positive and negative risks. This will lead to blurry visibility and high uncertainty for the project leaders.

One of my friends who was a project scheduler at the time told me that he was once involved with a multimillion-dollar project which never had more than ten open negative risks in their risk register throughout the project. The goal of the project was to build a system that included a wide range of components. They had many partners and stakeholders. For such a project, it is rare to have only ten risks. Not surprisingly, he said that the number of their issues increased to over one hundred as they moved through to project implementation. This is clearly indicative of very poor risk management.

However, the root cause laid in the existence of a low trust project environment. As I discussed this in more detail with him, I found that both the project team and stakeholders were reluctant to share risk-related information simply because they did not trust each other.

Other Project Plan Components

Lack of (or low) trust in the project environment hinders the exchange of honest and transparent information as the project team plans for other components of the project, including assessment of the tools, capabilities and skills (human resources management), quality, change, procurement, and stakeholder and communication management. This is how plans end up as merely words on paper and how the planning loses its momentum.

***

Benjamin Franklin stated it nicely, "By failing to prepare, you prepare to fail" (n.d.). Effective planning is the first step toward successful project management. You need to collaborate with your management/sponsor, project team, users, and other key stakeholders to produce a reliable plan. You cannot do it without building trust as the first step.

Chapter Two

Trust and Project Execution

In the planning phase, you work with your stakeholders to identify your target location, route, vehicle, and tool to navigate toward your destination. In the execution phase, using driving as an analogy, it is time to click *start* on your navigation screen, push the ignition button, and start driving toward your target with your team. The difference compared to a real driving scenario is that you will not utilize all the controls on your own. You may only use the navigation to guide your team through the roads. Every member of your team will have their own single control (gearshift, steering wheel, gas pedal, brake lights, etc.) in their hands.

As a result, in order for your vehicle to move efficiently and effectively, you need to coordinate and rely on each other. You will also need to rely on others, including other drivers, motorcycle riders, cyclists, pedestrians (external stakeholders) outside your vehicle. Likewise, the lower that your confidence is in your team and others, the more hazards and traffic you will encounter during your journey.

Project execution is an integral part of your project. This is where you use the project plan as the baseline to create the target product and/or service. As the project manager, you must ensure that every team member completes their work effectively. You coordinate with your team on the project work, regularly communicate progress with your stakeholders, and prevent issues, roadblocks, and impediments along the way. You also provide your team with the knowledge and support they need to complete their work, identify lessons-learned, and continuously improve as you move forward. The following lists some of the questions you might frequently and repeatedly ask as you are monitoring and controlling the project execution:

1. Is the work being done according to plan (on time, within budget, in scope)?
2. Are we delivering more or less than required?
3. Is the work being done effectively and efficiently?
4. Have we acquired enough resources?
5. Do our current resources have the relevant skills, capabilities, and tools to do the work? If not, how can we assist them (help develop skills and capabilities, provide tools, etc.)?
6. Are we communicating sufficiently with the project stakeholders? If not, how can we improve it?
7. Is the team receiving the information they need to do the work?
8. Are we engaging stakeholders effectively? If not, how can we improve?
9. Are we minimizing or preventing risks, issues, and defects? If not, how can we improve our measures?

10. Do we need to make any changes to the project baselines (scope, quality, budget, time) to remain relevant?
11. Is the team motivated, interested, committed, and transparent?

The answers you get from these questions will help you gauge if you are moving in the right direction and making progress. This will maximize the chance of your project being successful. Who will answer these questions for you? In a small project, you might be able to find some (not all) of the answers on your own.

But when you have a large and complex project, you must depend on your team for every question. The last question, "Is the team motivated, interested, committed, and transparent?" is particularly important as it will indicate if the project leaders have created the proper, healthy environment for the team to work in. When any of the four key elements (motivation, interest, commitment, and transparency) is lacking, there is a serious trust issue within your project. Fold your sleeves and start working on it!

Motivation

If one of your team members hits a million-dollar lottery today, will they come to work at least for a smooth handover? If the answer is no, then that team member does not have the right (intrinsic) motivation to work in the project. Extrinsic motivations such as a salary increase, bonus, or a trip to Vegas are just as good as meeting the minimum requirements to hit those targets. But to ensure a successful execution, you need more than this. You want your team to go above and beyond in order to create a quality product and/or service. This is done by ensuring that the team feels recognized, appreciated, and valued (intrinsically motivated). This is possible only in a trusted environment.

Interest

Is your team interested in the type of product and/or service your project aims to create? Are they interested in the whole project or only care about the piece that they need to create? To ensure on-going learning and continuous improvement in your team, it is vital for your project team to remain interested and focused on the project. High trust in your project will arouse the interest of your project team. Low trust, on the other hand, will diminish the interest of your team members, ultimately leading to unhappiness, low morale, and a poor outcome.

Commitment

Are your team members committed to you, other team members, and the project? Being interested and motivated contributes to your team's commitment, but it takes more than that to keep your team fully committed. If your team members are not committed, a similar project (with the same interests and motivations) might attract them to leave your project work unfinished even for minor incentive differences. Continuous appreciation and recognition in a trusted atmosphere will ensure your team remains committed until the end of the project. I have seen project managers spending most of their time backfilling project roles; and I am sure that you do not want to experience the same thing. Remember, trust is all it takes.

Transparency

Getting the right answers for your project execution questions is not achievable in the absence of a transparent environment. You do not want rosy facts and polished reports. You do not want your team to hide any issues, defects, or potential risks. You want to have full and clear visibility over your project. Building trust is the only way to create transparency. Your team members should not be afraid to share bad news with the mindset that it will undermine their own performance. Having a trusting environment will ensure you prevent many of the avoidable issues and risks in a timely manner. On the other hand, no trust, no transparency.

***

Trust comes at the heart of project execution. It is the fuel that keeps your team energized, focused, and happy. It also helps the information flow smoothly and transparently among your project stakeholders. It is a freeway all the way to your end goal.

Chapter Three

Trust and Monitoring & Controlling

As you most likely understand, project monitoring and controlling are integrated with every part of the project. Monitoring and controlling are constant from project inception to completion. We cannot segregate them from any part of the project work or phase. My discussion in the previous chapter, Trust and Project Execution, involved project monitoring and controlling from the project manager's perspective. In this section, we will focus on how trust influences effective self-monitoring and controlling. When your team's trust level is high, every member of your team will continuously ask the following questions:

1. Am I doing my work according to plan (on time, within budget, in scope)?
2. Am I doing my work effectively and efficiently?
3. Am I collaborating well with my teammates?
4. Do I have the skills, capabilities, and tools to do the work? If not, how can I improve my skills and capabilities, and how can I obtain the tools?
5. Am I communicating effectively with the project stakeholders? If not, how can I improve it?

6. Do I have the information I need? If I do not, how can I obtain it?

7. Is the team getting the information they need from me to do their work?

8. Am I making honest efforts to ensure quality, prevent issues and defects, and identify potential risks?

9. Do I need to make any changes to make my performance better?

10. Do I need any help? If so, who can I ask for help?

11. Does my team enjoy working with me? If not, what can I do to make it better?

12. What else can I do to contribute to my team's success?

In a low trust environment, your team members will lack intrinsic motivation, interest, and commitment to think outside the box. When there is low trust, your team's priority will be to meet the minimum job requirements only to the extent to keep their paychecks coming. On the other hand, when trust is high, your team members will proactively monitor and control their performance to ensure they remain effective and efficient team players. This will significantly save you time and effort, and help you detect and prevent project issues ahead of the time. Because your team members care about the success of the group in a high trust team, they will constantly self-monitor and control to make sure they (as individual players) are *doing the right things* and *doing them right*.

Are You Doing the Right Things?

As team players, your team members will ask this question to make sure they are doing what they are supposed to do to contribute to and create their part of the product and/or service. They want to make sure that their inputs create the desired outputs that meet the project requirements and the users' needs. This assessment will help them identify and segregate value-added from non-value-added activities at the individual level. They will continuously assess and test the outputs to confirm functionality according to the quality requirements. As a result, you will see the following benefits at the project level:

- The risk of scope creep is minimized. Project activities are being performed in scope
- Project deliverables meet the quality requirements
- Integration (of subsystems/parts) is seamless
- Time, money, and resources are used efficiently
- Risks and issues are identified in time
- Flow of information is effective
- Stakeholders are engaged effectively

Doing the right things is an important step to your project success as it keeps your team focused on the value-added activities. Once your team knows they are doing the right things, what they will think about next is whether they are doing them right.

Are You Doing Things Right?

Is this the best way (effective and efficient) to do my work? Is there a better way to do it? These are some of the questions that your team members will ponder and might even worry about to make sure they add the most value to the team they trust. What comes at the core of this self-assessment is the element of thinking outside the box. This is where your team will go above and beyond not only to deliver a fine product and/or service to your client, but also to do this in the shortest amount of time and in the most cost-effective way. Besides the benefits listed above, this assessment will create the following benefits to your project and organization:

- Project work (in all aspects) is continuously improved
- Time and effort are significantly saved
- Stakeholder satisfaction level goes above expectations

***

When there is trust in a team, project team members take a proactive approach to continuously assess their own performance and make sure they are contributing to the project's success. They also strive to identify opportunities to improve performance and save money and effort for the project. This makes the project manager's job a lot easier to monitor and control the overall project. Without trust, project managers will have to spend a lot of unnecessary and unavailable time to collect project data, confirm, and reconfirm the validity of every piece of information. Transparency will be a core issue. Resolving (rather than preventing) problems will make up most of the project manager's day-to-day job. In other words, the project manager will be forced into a reactive mode versus a proactive mode.

Chapter Four

Trust and Project Closing

Your project inception and planning stages go well, your execution is a success with effective monitoring and controlling, and now it is time to close the project. One might say, "Well, at this stage we have completed most of the project, so it's really not so important to focus on trust issues…it is time to hand over the product/service and simply close the project, right?" It is, in fact, on the contrary. Project closing is a crucial stage for you and your team to tie the ends of trust as you are concluding the project.

A loose knot could ruin the strong ties of trust you've already built through the previous phases of the project with your stakeholders. By showing high trust, you create an opportunity to sustain your long-term strong relationship with your stakeholders. Not only do you ensure a successful conclusion to your project, but you also secure trust in future projects with which you will be involved. Most importantly, you build on your credibility in the personal and professional community.

As you close out the project with your team, you need answers to the following key questions:

1. Does the final product and/or service meet the latest requirements/users' needs as per the project scope? Does it meet the business needs?

2. Does the project meet the project completion criteria?

3. Were the metrics used to measure project progress against project baselines (scope, quality, cost, and time) effective?

4. Was the project management approach (including management of all project knowledge areas from project integration to stakeholder management) effective?

5. Did the project meet the cost, quality, scope, and time objectives?

6. Were there any variances? If so, how were they managed?

7. Were there any risks and issues? If so, how were they addressed?

8. Was there any evidence to support our answers? If so, what are they?

9. Are there any lessons-learned? If so, what are they, and how can we learn from them for future projects?

Trust within your team and stakeholders validates your successful transition of the final product and/or service, guarantees the successful delivery of a comprehensive project completion report to relevant project stakeholders, and, most importantly, ensures you draw an inclusive list of lessons learned to add to your company's knowledge base for application to similar future projects.

Final Product/Service Transition

Transition of the final product and/or service is usually not a one step process. There may be many steps to take and multiple stakeholders to involve. Depending on the type of the project, the final product and/or service may include a hyper-care period that may last for several weeks or months.

A hyper-care period is a timeframe of a few weeks or months after product and/or service delivery to the client. During this period, a dedicated technical team of the project works closely with the users to make sure the product and/or service functions properly. Intensive care of the product and/or service and a swift response to users' and clients' inquiries during this period is of essence to the project's successful closure.

In addition, the technical team assigned during this period may include experts from other departments/functions of the company who may have not been involved in the development of the product and/or service. Using trust as the primary tool speeds up the process to make the team perform effectively. In fact, as the project manager, you should have already built strong trust with these key stakeholders prior to entering the hyper-care phase.

The final product and/or service transition may also include handover to the client's operations department. In this process, your project team will need to coordinate closely with the maintenance and operations team of the client. Trust comes at the core of your successful coordination and handover to this team.

Product and/or service transition may involve many other intensive activities, which is usually a complex process. It involves a wide range of stakeholders (some of whom may not have been working with you in the previous phases of the project). It is also a risky process for both your project and the client as it may involve changes to their current operations. To minimize the risks, make the transition smooth, and increase the odds of success in your project, it is important that you put trust at the heart of your transition activities.

Project Completion Report (Final Report)

The project completion report is where you officially document your project's accomplishments (or unfulfillments, God forbid!). On a high level, the project completion report is where you confirm (with evidence) that you have met the project's goals and objectives. You also provide details of any variances between the outcome and the project plan, including quality, scope, cost, and time baselines. You describe why and how these variances occurred and how your project team responded to them. You also describe your approach to, and the outcomes of, risk and issue management.

To prepare the final report, you must rely heavily on your project team, subject matter experts, and other stakeholders. Your goal in this process (as in any other undertaking) is to collect reliable and valid information. As this is your final report, and the fact that you may not have any chance to rectify, any flawed information could have dire consequences to the project and your credibility. How do you ensure your team and stakeholders provide you with accurate information to feed into this report? The first step is to make sure you, your team, and the stakeholders trust each other.

Lessons Learned

Identifying and documenting lessons-learned is the vital part of the project. Although this step is part of the project closing, the process for identifying and documenting lessons learned starts right from the inception of the project. As you are monitoring and continuously improving the project work, you capture lessons learned. During this part, in general, you identify 1) what you have done well, 2) what you could do better, 3) what you could stop doing, and 4) what you could start doing. Your and your team's observations are critical to identifying these four lessons-learned components. To share their observations objectively and without any fears, your project needs an environment of high trust. Any feeling of mistrust and fear could impede the transparency of this key step.

***

Trust remains a key player during the project closing phase. In this process, you will not only work with your current team and stakeholders, but also start interfacing with other relevant workstreams and partners (such as maintenance and operations, customer service, legal department, accounting department, technical SMEs, end users, etc.) in your and/or your client's company. Trust will be the primary accelerator of building an effective relationship with all the key players involved in this vital phase.

Chapter Five

Trust and Agility

Agile, without any surprise, is a popular term in the world of information technology project management today. According to multiple studies cited in *The Project Manager's Guide to Mastering Agile*, adoption of agile project management in industries is on the rise (Cobb, 2015). There are many reasons that trigger an adaptive (e.g., agile) project management approach to take prominence. Change in the nature of projects (emergence of new industries such as mobile, e-commerce, small to large scale IT projects, and a wide range of projects), rapid advancement of technology (Cobb, 2015), increasing customer power (due to increased competition and a wide range of product choices), and fierce business competition (race on price and speed to market) are among the key drivers that prompt the need for an adaptive project management methodology.

How does adaptive project management help achieve these goals? Adaptive project management encourages prioritizing four key project factors (over others): teamwork and collaboration, quality product and/or service, customer/client continuous engagement, and embracing change. *Agile Manifesto*, which was published in the early 2000s, is based on these four guiding principles of agile project management. The manifesto states the following:

> "We are uncovering better ways of developing software by doing it and helping others do it. Through this work we have come to value:
>
> - Individuals and interactions over processes and tools
> - Working software over comprehensive documentation
> - Customer collaboration over contract negotiation
> - Responding to change over following a plan
>
> That is, while there is value in the items on the right, we value the items on the left more" (Beck et al., 2001).

These key priorities enable project managers to adapt the project management method based on the nature of the project, keep pace with technology advancements (as agile always embraces change), increase customer satisfaction, and maximize competitive advantage by speeding up the time to market through the focus on product (rather than unnecessary bureaucracies and documentations).

Where does trust come in agile methodology? By just looking at the agile manifesto above, you may have already determined that trust becomes even more important where there is more agility. You cannot incorporate any of the four core values without having a strong trustful environment.

Individuals and Interactions

Agile project management underlines the importance of empowering every individual to play their role in the project in a flexible and adaptive approach. By doing so, it minimizes any overemphasis on tools and processes, particularly when they do not serve the purpose. You can only empower your team members when you extend your trust to them. They also need to trust that you will support them when they make decisions independently. Recurring failures and poor performance are inevitable when team members are empowered in the absence of sufficient trust. It is, however, important to understand that empowering your team members is one of the signs of extending your trust to them. I have more to say on empowering in the second part of this book.

Agile also focuses on effective interactions among your project stakeholders. Effective interaction is about communicating information transparently. Do you think that your team members will be willing to share information transparently if they do not trust you and others on the team? I doubt it.

Working Product

Agile focuses on the working product and/or service rather than non-value-added documentation. By doing so, it ensures that the project client and end-users have sufficient visibility over the product and/or service being developed. This will lead to the end product and/or service being in line with the end-users' needs.

Producing unnecessary extensive documentation distracts your and your team's attention from producing a working product and/or service. Have you ever been involved in a project when you had to make sure you had a written record for every project correspondence and/or decision? If yes, this may have been an extreme situation of overemphasis on documentation. Why do you have to document every move in the project? From my experience, this is a clear sign of low trust in a team.

I was once part of a project that required documenting every direction from the senior management and project client. Verbal direction was not valid because there was a history of denial by senior management when the project had encountered failures due to their decisions. The project managers and teams were instead held solely responsible for the failures. In such a situation, the same problem extends to the project team. No team member will be willing to show flexibility or make a move unless they have a recorded direction from their project leader.

Trust is a vital factor to minimize focus on excessive documentation and to maximize the team's focus on producing a functional product and/or service. Without trust, rigidity is inevitable.

Customer Collaboration and Change

Continuous customer engagement is a top priority in agile project management. The relationship between the project and the customer is based on a trustful partnership with a win-win mindset. The goal of the project is to meet the customer's needs which may change during the project. Therefore, "agile processes harness change for the customer's competitive advance" (Beck et al., 2001) rather than limiting and/or controlling change. Continuous customer engagement and incorporating change effectively require a high trust relationship between the project team and customer.

***

Trust comes at the core of agility in project management. Without this imperative element, you will not be able to create an empowered team, build a transparent environment for interactions, and focus on producing a functional product and/or service. In addition, continuous engagement with customers and embracing change make trust the cornerstone of effective project management.

Trust is an essential element in every part of the project. It helps your project move smoothly and in the right direction. It helps you and your team identify and avoid risks and issues in a timely manner.

In particular, trust helps:

- Create a collaborative relationship between the project team and other stakeholders
- Avoid imposed and unrealistic project targets and baselines
- Create an environment of transparency
- Amplify visibility over project risks and issues
- Keep project teams motivated, interested, and committed
- Minimize non-value-added activities
- Ensure effectiveness and efficiency
- Enhance customer engagement
- Maximize continuous improvement in your project

An environment of low trust raises the prospects of project challenges and failures to a significant degree.

At this point you might say, "I now understand the significance of trust in project success. Tell me how to build it." I have dedicated the remaining sections of this book to discuss how to build trust in your project based on a combination of my personal experience and extensive literature review.

Part Two

Building Trust in Your Team

"I came to believe that leaders ...are good because they are willing...to trust....[I]f you are a leader, the people you've counted on will help you up...and the people who count on you need you on your feet" (McChrystal, 2011). As the project manager and leader, you play the central role in building trust in your team. You make the first step to inspire trust by showing your confidence in your team. When you rely upon each one of your team members, they show commitment and loyalty to the project. You make them feel responsible and motivated to keep your trust. This is how they will put genuine effort into performing better to confirm that you are right about them, that they are trustworthy.

Moreover, they will trust you and other team members in return. Years of lab experiments by the prominent neuroscientist Paul J. Zak (2017) indicates that extending trust to others increases their love hormone (oxytocin), thereby rewarding their brains for helping and treating others in the same manner. Trust is both reciprocal and contagious (in a positive way, of course!).

Over my years of exploration and trial, I have found that *empowering* team members is the core of building trust within a team. To empower effectively, you need to accomplish seven key objectives. To make it easier for you to remember, I have formulated these seven objectives to make the acronym **EMPOWER**. They are 1) **E**stablishing a shared vision, 2) **M**anaging expectations, 3) **P**romoting creativity, 4) **O**ptimizing stakeholder collaboration, 5) **W**alking the talk, 6) **E**liciting feedback continuously, and 7) **R**eadjusting behavior, as needed. Nevertheless, before we discuss EMPOWER, let us review some of the key foundation stones upon which we build trust with others.

Chapter Six

The Foundations of Building Trust with Others

Several years ago, I came across a vibrant program director whom I will call Tom. When I started working with Tom, I found him to be just the kind of leader I was looking for. He apparently trusted and empowered everyone on his team. His approach kept everyone in the program highly engaged, committed, and united. He had an open-door policy and loved to hear creative ideas. He would stand strong against *outsiders* and not let anyone, not even his own boss, point negatively toward his team. Everyone on the team really enjoyed working with Tom. He was *the* role model.

After a few months, the company's president decided to move Tom to a different (but better) role. He was given only three weeks to wrap up with his current team. Tom's new role was in a different workstream and did not require him to engage with anyone in his new capacity. As soon as Tom learned about the president's decision, the team started to notice a gradual change in Tom's behavior toward the team. His open-door policy changed, and we had to make sure he had nothing on his immediate plate before knocking on his door. During his last two weeks with the program, Tom only spent less than twenty

40

percent of his time with the team. Most of his time was spent meeting people he was supposed to work with in his new role. Even before moving to his new office, he had fully moved his vibrance to his new team. This led to a serious impact on our team's morale. No one on the team trusted Tom anymore. In addition, it took a lot of time and effort for our team to build trust with the new program director because Tom had not left a good impression behind.

What was lacking in Tom's character? Although Tom seemed to have built a strong relationship with his team based on trust, it was not durable. In fact, the foundations, such as authenticity and integrity, upon which Tom had built trust, was vulnerable. Trust is built on a set of strong foundations. If the foundations are not solid, it is almost impossible to build and maintain trust with others. A simple force may impact and reverse your whole journey, just like in Tom's case. In this chapter, we will explore some of the key foundations that give your *trust building* stability and durability against any detrimental events.

Foundation 1: Self-Trust

The primary prerequisite for extending trust to others is trusting yourself. Over years of my personal experience and observations, I have concluded that a project manager's self-trust is based on the following five key pillars: 1) right intensions and actions, 2) consistency, 3) cognition, 4) project management and leadership expertise, and 5) product knowledge. These attributes are either manifest in your character (such as right intentions and actions, consistency, and cognition) or your professional background (such as project management and leadership expertise, and product knowledge).

1) Right Intentions and Actions

For right intentions and right actions, I have taken the inspiration from Buddha's Noble Eightfold Path. Buddha describes the right intentions (having the right thought free of ill-will and full of good will) (Bodhi, 1984, 1994) and right actions (based on ethical conduct that produces the desired outcomes) among the eight best practices of reaching high morality in his Noble Eightfold Path (Bodhi, 1984, 1994). We cannot trust ourselves if we do not take the actions based on the motives that produce the desired outcomes. The level of one's integrity defines whether one strives for the right intentions and actions. The following questions can be key in determining the rightness of your intentions and actions in a project:

- What is my motive to work as the project leader/manager (or any other role) in this project? What are my extrinsic and intrinsic motivations? Which side is heavier, intrinsic or extrinsic motivation? (Hint: the heavier one's intrinsic motivation the better chances their intensions and actions are more relevant).

42

- Does my current role fit my career goals? (Hint: if one's current role is just a job to keep the paycheck flowing in, then one might not have the right motivation to strive for intentions and actions that are best for the whole team).

- Do I care about others in the project? How much do I care about them versus myself? (Hint: the more you care about others, the greater the chance your intentions and actions are more relevant).

- Do I care about success of every individual, the team, project, company, or just myself? What is the order of priority? (Hint: the more you care about success of others, the greater the chance your intensions and actions are more relevant).

- Am I able to take the actions that I intend? (Hint: the more capable you are in taking actions in line with your intensions, the better your self-trust will be).

2) Consistency

What if one has the right intentions but takes the right actions only randomly? Randomness creates uncertainty and ambiguity which will significantly impact your trust on yourself. To build self-trust, it is important to ensure your actions are consistent. You may have heard a common expression that *consistent actions create consistent results.*

I really like cooking and would like to serve my family and friends with some delicious meals of their choice. However, I do not trust myself in this joyful task because I am not able to produce the same results each time I cook. The root cause falls in my inability to follow the same process every time. I have experienced this with three groups of my friends (who presumably have the same taste in general). The first group still talks about how delicious the *Palaw* (rice dish) I once cooked for them was. The second group of my friends remember the bad taste from the same recipe. The third group have tasted both sides of the extreme! The latter group fortunately (or unfortunately) had the chance to taste my dish more than once. I have given up my self-trust on cooking for a long time because I cannot consistently cook a good dish.

The same analogy can be applied to project management and leadership. It is your consistent behaviors that help produce consistent results. And results are important because they strengthen your ability to build and keep trust with others (Covey & Merrill, 2018).

3) Cognition

How do you perceive the world and the people around you? How do you learn and apply new learning? How do you make and justify your decisions? The way you think and make decisions using cognitive processes identifies your answers to these questions. The relevance of your thinking, reasoning, and decision-making processes is determined by the outcome they produce to build and maintain trust with your stakeholders.

To assess your cognitive skills, Bloom's revised taxonomy (Anderson & Krathwohl) is a good place to start. As depicted in the figure below (Vanderbilt University Center for Teaching), the framework divides our cognitive processes into six key categories that describe how we learn and apply knowledge to make our day-to-day decisions.

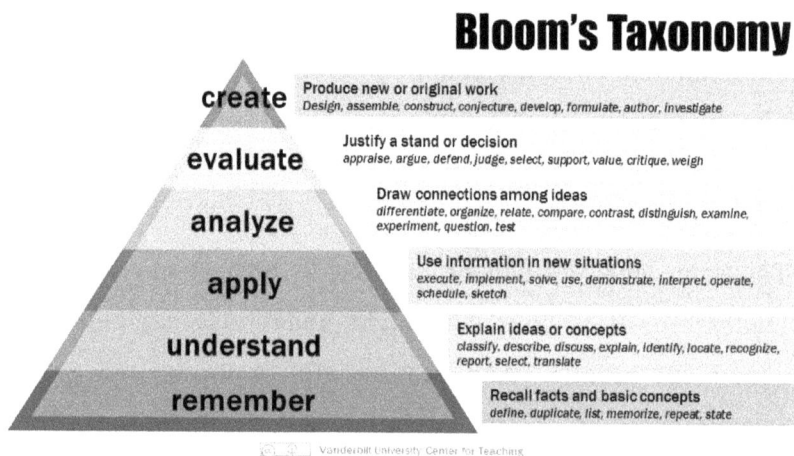

Bloom's Taxonomy

create — Produce new or original work
Design, assemble, construct, conjecture, develop, formulate, author, investigate

evaluate — Justify a stand or decision
appraise, argue, defend, judge, select, support, value, critique, weigh

analyze — Draw connections among ideas
differentiate, organize, relate, compare, contrast, distinguish, examine, experiment, question, test

apply — Use information in new situations
execute, implement, solve, use, demonstrate, interpret, operate, schedule, sketch

understand — Explain ideas or concepts
classify, describe, discuss, explain, identify, locate, recognize, report, select, translate

remember — Recall facts and basic concepts
define, duplicate, list, memorize, repeat, state

Vanderbilt University Center for Teaching

Figure 6.1: Bloom's Taxonomy, Vanderbilt University Center for Teaching

In project management, your cognitive ability to develop ideas, identify and examine alternatives, utilize knowledge and experience effectively, and understand and remember concepts help you make effective decisions that your team can rely upon.

4) Project Management and Leadership Expertise

Competence is a vital element in building your self-trust. Competence consists of two core elements, capabilities and results, both helping you build your trustworthiness (Covey & Merrill, 2018). Project management and leadership expertise makes up the essential part of your competence that will help you produce consistent results and build trust with your stakeholders. As the project manager and/or leader, you need to be adept across both managing and leading teams and projects throughout the project lifecycle. Lack of confidence in this core area will substantially negatively impact both your and others' trust on you. One can be a person of high integrity and have great cognitive skills, but without sufficient project management knowledge and skills, self-trust is almost impossible to build and maintain in the role of project manager and/or leader.

However, building trust through your competence does not mean that you must be equally competent in all areas of project management and leadership. It requires you to be honest about your abilities, vulnerabilities, knowledge and unawareness, and ask for help where and when you need it (Feltman, 2009).

5) Product Knowledge

Product knowledge is another key part of your competence. You do not need to have deep technical knowledge of a product and/or service your project aims to build (unless you are a one-man army of the project), but you do need to have sufficient working knowledge of the product and/or service (including its application, functions, features, uses, and other relevant elements) to lead the project from point A to point B. The sufficiency of your knowledge of the product and/or service is determined by the context in which you are managing and leading the project. Lack of adequate knowledge can put you in a vulnerable position and can lower your self-trust.

To build trust with others successfully, you need to make sure you trust yourself within the role that you are playing in the project. Having the right intentions, taking appropriate decisions by using relevant cognitive processes, and ensuring adequate project management, leadership and product knowledge while acknowledging your gaps can help build your self-trust effectively.

Foundation 2: Emotional Intelligence

During the course of a project, you and your team may encounter a wide range of stressful situations that could impact your emotions. These emotions might lead to certain unfavorable reactions impacting trust in the team. Even one reaction emerging from negative emotions such as anger or sadness could damage the roots of trust within a group. In my first project management job as assistant project manager, I reported to a project manager who was highly skilled and very honest. However, the manager was not able to control her anger in certain stressful situations. Everyone on the team trusted her until they experienced some form of her anger. By the end of her designation as the leader of the project, there were only a few people who could bear to work with her again.

Everyone is susceptible to emotions, and in different levels of degree. A person with high Emotional Intelligence (EI), also known as Emotional Quality (EQ), that was first suggested and explored in-depth by the prominent author and science journalist Daniel Goleman (1995), has the ability to understand and manage emotions of self and others in every situation. Drawing from a study, Goleman concluded that people with high EQ have better job performance. In fact, EQ increases the chances of successful performance more than Intellectual Quality (IQ) does. It is possible to be a low performer and have a high IQ, but it is rare to have low performance with a high EQ. Bradberry and Greaves (2009) confirmed the rate of low performers with high EQ to be at only 20 percent.

What is good about EQ is that it is improvable. You can improve your EQ to better understand your emotions and those of others and manage them effectively. A low EQ can lead to reactions opposite to your intentions, thereby possibly leaving long-lasting damage to your trustful relationship with the team.

Foundation 3: Objectivity

I used to work with a program director who shared a close ethnic background with two team members. One of these team members struggled with performance issues. This was known to the whole program team. One day as I walked into the office, I learned that the mentioned team member was promoted to the role of senior project manager. This was unexpected and shocked everyone on the team. The team attributed the decision to be mainly influenced by the program director's ethnic bias.

Before this event, the program director was known for his great leadership and relationship building skills. There were no negative politics and trust was the core of the team's motives. After the event, trust gradually faded and was ultimately replaced by negative politics, the culture of blaming, and the mission of survival. Although the program director later moved on as he was not able to recover the team's trust, the team's poor performance remained as the major issue for the rest of the program and caused significant costs to the program and organization.

Objectivity is vital in building trust because a minor visible bias could undermine the validity of rationality behind your current and future decisions, making it hard for your team to trust you. The project team and stakeholders will believe in you if your decisions are impartial, free of biases including external influences, your opinions, personal feelings, and emotions. You need to identify any of these biases that could potentially influence your actions and apply a relevant objective decision-making approach to minimize them. Involving your team and stakeholders in your decisions, where possible, for instance, is an effective way to maximize objectivity and ensure trust.

Foundation 4: Intercultural Competence

Intercultural competence is your ability to communicate and behave effectively with people who come from a different culture than yours (Cultural Detective, n.d.). You may have heard the famous saying, "Treat others the way you wish to be treated," known as *The Golden Rule.* I remember an interesting anecdote from the book *Creating a Greater Whole* that depicts a slightly different view on treating others. It talks about treating others the way they (not you) wish to be treated (Schwartz, 2018). This statement made more sense to me as I reflected on my own experience of having worked with people from a wide range of cultural backgrounds.

When I worked in my country of birth, Afghanistan, there were a few times that my new western male colleagues tried to shake hands with (and a couple of times hug) my Afghan female colleagues. Although some of my colleagues were ok with it, others did not take this behavior as a sign of respect. Obviously, my western colleagues had no intention but to show respect. In fact, they wanted to treat my colleagues the way they wished to be treated.

In most western cultures, shaking hands (or hugging and kissing on the cheek) between friends and colleagues from opposite genders is a part of the greeting etiquette. Some cultures, on the other hand, such as practicing Muslims, perceive handshakes, hugging, and kissing between the opposite genders (unless they are a spouse *(mahram)* or a family member who they are unlawful to marry against their religious and cultural values. If someone is not aware of this key norm and attempts to shake hands or hug an opposite gender in the Muslim culture, they inadvertently show disrespect, which in turn leads to a lack of trust.

Today teams are more diverse than they were in the past, and moving toward the future they will be even more. As diversity expands, intercultural competence takes more prominence. This key competency will enable us to understand and treat others as they prefer to be treated, therefore leading to greater trustful relationships.

***

The strength of your trust with others is based on four key foundations: self-trust, emotional intelligence, objectivity, and intercultural competence. To ensure self-trust, you need to have the right intentions, take the right actions, build on your cognitive skills, and enhance your project management, leadership, and product knowledge. To recognize and manage your emotions and those of others, you should build on your EQ. Understanding and minimizing your biases is also vital to maximize impartiality in your decisions, which will boost your team's and stakeholders' trust in you. Finally, given the increasing diverse cultures in teams, understanding cultural values of people who are culturally different than you is important to enhance your effective communication and behavior.

Chapter Seven

EMPOWER to Build Trust

When I started my career in project management as a project assistant, the initial feedback from my first boss suggested that I exceeded expectations in one part of my performance—following processes and accomplishing tasks exactly as I was told to do. Being at an entry level position and given the job market competition at the time, during the first few months I was extremely excited just to have a job. My goal was to ensure the security of my employment by meeting expectations of the job as I was directed. I was motivated and interested. My boss and I had no complaints from each other. After a few months, I started to realize the principles behind doing certain tasks. I started to feel more ingenious.

Wanting to do my job better, one day I came up with a few suggestions that required minor changes to the process but evidently increased the efficiency and effectiveness of the tasks. I presented the proposal to my boss with quite some excitement. However, he refused my proposal right away without telling me why. In fact, he began to control the process and manage me even more closely. I could not make even a minor decision independently. My motivation and interest declined significantly. I did not enjoy my job anymore. This feeling suddenly reminded me of the excitement and passion I had for the job when I met my second boss. He was on the opposite spectrum. He praised me and rewarded me for every new idea. He gave me the freedom to make decisions. He was always by my side and never let me be fearful of mistakes. I excelled in my role and got promoted to the role of junior project manager in just six months. It was during that time that project management was reaffirmed as the right career path for me.

Today, reflecting back on these two types of bosses in the early years of my project management career, I have learned to differentiate a good leader with a *not so good leader* using one key identifier, *the degree to which they empower their followers*. In fact, empowering teams, where possible, is a key trust principle (Thornton, 2008).

When you empower your team members, you achieve three primary objectives: 1) extending your trust, 2) building on confidence, motivation, and commitment of each team member, and 3) creating transparency within your team. All these elements in turn contribute to building an environment of high trust in every team.

1) Extending Trust

When you empower your team, you give them the freedom and authority to make certain decisions to do their work. This is one indication that you trust your team. As discussed earlier, trust is mutual. Extending your trust is the initial vital step to building a strong relationship with your team members. Noble Prize winner Ernest Hemingway (n.d.) puts it nicely, "The best way to find out if you can trust somebody is to trust them." And when you trust your team, in return they will trust you and each other. This is how a high trust environment is established.

However, extending trust comes with certain risks, particularly when you are dealing with new individuals or teams. The author of the New York Times Bestseller *Speed of Trust*, Stephen M.R. Covey (2018) suggests extending trust wisely by balancing between your distrust (suspicion) and blind trust (gullibility) to ensure you have accounted for the associated risks of trusting. You can do this by adjusting the degree to which you empower each of your team members.

2) Confidence, Motivation, and Commitment

Have you ever thought about why humans pursue money, power, and status? Happiness might be an instant answer. But when I reflect and think about life, it goes beyond happiness. If happiness was the only reason, then why do we tend to want more and more of the money, power, and status? We will achieve enduring happiness when we feel content with what we already have. But how do we feel content? I believe we feel so when we overcome one of our innermost desires of feeling important. We are happy when we are important, and we feel important when we have power and/or status.

You might have figured out by now that empowering your team achieves exactly the goal above. When your team feels important, it makes them confident in what they do. They feel that their work counts and is valuable. They also feel motivated because they want to do their best to get more empowered, thereby feeling even more important. Finally, they will stay committed to you and the project because they do not want to lose such a positive response to their inner desires.

Some of your team members, having stronger desires for feeling important than others, might get so motivated that they want a similar job like yours. I do not only think it is harmless for your project but also beneficial to the whole organization if they prove that they serve to rise to that status. As a leader, it is essentially part of your job to pave the way for your team's professional development. However, if any of your team members use unfair routes to move up the ladder, this is, among other things, a trust issue that you have to address.

3) Transparency

When I started a project in 2011 to develop learning resource centers in some education institutions in Afghanistan, we decided to hire part-time resource center coordinators who had experience working in the same institution. With this strategy, I aimed to ensure efficiency in communication and stakeholder management as the coordinators coming from the same organization knew how to communicate and influence leadership decisions in the best interests of the project. This way we did not have to invest in time and effort to build trust between coordinators and institutions.

However, one thing I neglected to initially do was to empower these coordinators to make certain decisions and commitments to the institution leadership independently. On the other hand, they wanted to have at least the same importance (if not more) for the leaders they used to work for directly in the past. Missing the opportunity to empower these coordinators not only did not stop them to make decisions on their own, but led them to make unrealistic commitments while withholding information regarding their correspondence from the rest of the project team. This caused several misunderstandings and challenges among the project team, project sponsors, and institutions during the preliminary stage of the project execution.

When I investigated the issue more in-depth, I found that the lack of empowerment was a major factor in impacting transparency within the coordinators' group. Transparency started increasing exponentially as soon as I granted the coordinators the power to make certain decisions. As a result, we were also able to resolve many of the existing relationship and communication challenges.

The coordinators demonstrated transparency when I empowered them because they wanted to keep my and the team's trust to remain empowered. And when there is transparency in a team, there is a sense of high trust. In fact, transparency is a critical quality that helps build trustful relationships (Bracey, 2010).

When you empower your team, you demonstrate that you trust them. This inspires a culture of mutual trust within your project. Each empowered individual will also feel important, thereby fulfilling their deep natural desires. This will make the individuals more confident, engaged, and committed. Finally, an empowered team will demonstrate high transparency, leading to a high trust project environment.

Empowerment is not a *one size fits all* process. The level of decision-making authority given to each team member should be based on their role, capabilities, and character. A project quality assurance manager, for instance, may be authorized to make quality-related decisions based on their expertise and track record. Any decision outside the realm of quality and the manager's capabilities should be made by a different team member who have those specific skills. The same principle applies to other project roles. As the project manager and/or leader, you should assess and assign the right level of authority to each team member and other project stakeholders.

Moreover, empowering, even if adjusted at the appropriate level, is not free of risks. The risks are particularly high in the following situations:

- There is a lack of shared vision within the team
- Stakeholder expectations are not clear and/or existing expectations change without control
- Creative thinking is minimized within the project
- There is minimal team collaboration
- The project leader indicates lack of accountability and fails to live with the core values
- There is a lack of constructive criticism within the team
- The project leader does not adapt their approach and strategy to ensure relevance

To address these challenges and empower your team successfully, apply the **EMPOWER** strategy:

1) **E**stablish a shared vision

2) **M**anage expectations

3) **P**romote creativity

4) **O**ptimize team collaboration

5) **W**alk the talk consistently

6) **E**licit feedback continuously

7) **R**eadjust as needed

I have designated the remaining chapters of this book to discuss these seven important steps to empower and build a high trust team in an effective way.

Chapter Eight

Establish a Shared Vision

Responses from close to a million people in a leadership survey suggest that one of the key challenges leaders face is portraying a vision that their followers could personally feel and connect with (Kouzes & Posner, 2009). When team members face such a lack of personal connection with their organization or the project's vision, they will not buy into it. This impacts the individuals' interest, motivation, and commitment, thereby leading to trust issues and performance challenges within the team.

Not long ago, I was involved in the implementation of an electronic tolling program in Virginia. The goal of the program was to minimize traffic congestion and save significant time for residents and daily commuters in the area. One of the program's technical team members used to commute for at least an hour and a half (one way). Although incredibly talented, feedback on his performance suggested that he was not engaged enough in the program.

As I was chatting with him informally one day, I found that the root cause of his low engagement laid in his disconnect from the goal of the program. He told me that the daily tolls priced by a similar program (in the same company) was so high that he could not financially afford it. He personally thought that charging tolls was more about making money than helping traffic. He did not believe in the program's end goal because he could not personally connect with it. In other words, he did not share the vision.

Lack of shared vision in a team could root in two major factors. Either the leader fails to articulate the vision in a way that depicts a clear, rather than blurry, desired picture of the future, or the team members do not find a common ground to relate to the vision. Both factors may trace back to the leader's leadership and communication skills.

Good leaders work closely with their teams to identify and agree on a shared vision, starting with the communication of the desired project's end-goal in a way that is comprehensible by all team members. This way the team can see and feel a sense of ownership (if it is what they are looking for) over the project vision because it is clear.

However, regardless of the clarity of the vision, some team members may simply not buy into it. This is also the leader's responsibility to identify and engage the right people. In my experience, if a team member does not relate to the project's vision, it is extremely difficult to build trust with and keep the individual engaged. It may be because, "it is not the work we remember with fondness, but the camaraderie [achieved through shared vision], how the group came together to get things done" (Sinek, 2014 & 2017, p. 279).

To establish a shared vision effectively, I suggest you apply the following principles:

1) Identify the right participants, including the project team and relevant stakeholders, to be involved in defining your project's vision
2) Clearly define and communicate the desired outcomes of the project
3) Plan and facilitate participatory workshops to define the project's core values and vision statement that is in line with personal goals and values
4) Ensure consensus and personally engage with those who may not immediately buy into the project's vision
5) Ensure the vision statement is comprehensive and defined in such a way that is motivational and touches personal feelings
6) Consistently communicate the vision statement to relevant stakeholders
7) Continuously assess performance and behavior against the project's vision to ensure alignment

The Right Stakeholders

Engaging the right stakeholders to define your project's vision is paramount to ensure a shared vision. The stakeholders are those who support, benefit from, or play a role in achieving your project's goals. It includes the project team, internal and external partners, executive management, clients, end-users, and customers. To involve the appropriate stakeholders, make sure you apply an effective approach to identify and analyze all individuals and groups who have a stake in your project. Neglecting to involve the relevant stakeholders, or involving the wrong ones, can have detrimental impact on building a shared vision.

The Project's Desired Outcomes

The desired outcomes are identified in the project charter at the initial phase of the project with input from the project's sponsor, client, end-users, and other relevant stakeholders. Make sure these outcomes are articulated in simple and noncontroversial language to your project team and stakeholders. To create a clear shared picture of the future, it is important that every team member understands why the project exists (e.g., business case), the project goals and objectives, the benefits that the project will create, project assumptions and constraints (including scope, quality, resource, and time constraints), and other relevant parameters. Encourage your team to ask questions and raise concerns until the desired outcomes are clear and appear realistic for all your team members.

Core Values and Vision

Defining your project's vision statement and core values are the most important steps in establishing a shared vision in your project. The project's vision statement portrays the project's desired end-goal while the core values are a set of guiding principles that will help your team reach the destination together safely and effectively.

To define both the vision statement and core values, involve every team member and relevant stakeholders where possible. This is how they will personalize and feel a sense of ownership toward the project's vision. To ensure effective involvement and contribution by your team members, plan and facilitate one or more workshops as appropriate. These workshops must have a participatory structure, giving a chance for every individual to speak and contribute. Remember to play the role of a facilitator, not a leader in these workshops. Set the ground rules to balance participation by all types of personalities, including extroverts and introverts. Continue these workshops until you have consensus on a concise vision statement and a set of core values.

Protesters

Sometimes you will have one or more outliers who will not agree with the general opinion of the project's vision and/or guiding principles. If you identify these individuals in your group, make sure you set a time with them offline to give them a chance to speak their minds. Try to understand why they oppose the rest of the group. There could be various reasons. They may have lower visibility over the project's vision and do not exactly understand what your project is trying to achieve, why and how. They might have a legitimate concern that you and others have not noticed. Identify the root cause and try to address it. If the project does not align with their personal goals, leave the door open and help them find another role/project that best suits their career path and interests. Not addressing the problem of the outliers can have a significant impact on the shared values and vision, trust, and ultimately the success of your project.

Concise Vision Statement

Dull and vague vision statements can only do as much as wasting your paper and printer ink and filling up your machine's memory by a few bytes, besides creating significant controversies within your project. Your vision statement should be in plain language, short and concise while realistic, vibrant, and motivational. The best vision statement makes the heart pound from excitement every time a project member reads it.

Communication

Some project managers might communicate the vision statement and core values, post them somewhere physically or electronically in the beginning of the project, and say, "The job is done." Not really. To make your project's vision and core values remain shared within your project, constantly communicate and remind the project members what the values and vision are. There are several ways to achieve this goal, including walking the talk (which we will discuss in Chapter 12), basing the project's performance metrics, rewards, and recognition system on vision and core values, capturing and disseminating success stories that include core values, and showing progress toward the vision. Communication is not simply saying it—it is showing it.

Assessment

Change is inevitable and you should embrace it. During the project, the client or end-users' expectations might change that will trigger a change in your project's focus and/or direction. Personal goals and interests of one or more members of your team might change. To ensure your project's vision and core values are relevant and aligned with your stakeholders' expectations, monitor, and assess regularly to identify such changes, and realign, as necessary.

***

Besides many benefits, shared vision helps your team make effective decisions. Without establishing a shared vision, empowering your team members can have adverse effects on your team's trust. Shared vision in a project exists when the project's vision and core values are in line with personal goals and values of every project member. To achieve this, you should communicate the project's desired outcomes and parameters unequivocally, involve all relevant stakeholders in defining your project's vision statement and core values through engaging workshops, ensure the project vision statement is defined in succinct language and arouses excitement, identify and address any outliers, consistently communicate the project vision and core values to project members, and continuously assess progress and realign your project, as needed.

Chapter Nine

<u>M</u>anage Expectations

"Trust development will only succeed when expectations are met and motives are clear" (Oldfield, 2017). Managing expectations effectively and maintaining a clear shared vision go hand-in-hand to avoid ambiguity and maximize trust between your project and the customer (end-users and/or the project client). The customer's expectations determine the requirements or user stories for *what* (the product or service) your project aims to build. In project management terms, this is known as the product requirements.

However, expectations of other groups of stakeholders such as the organization or executive sponsors (senior management), project team, partners, suppliers, and some other stakeholders may inform the *how* (to build the product or service) aspect of your project. You need to clearly understand and align expectations of these stakeholders in order to plan and apply relevant tools, techniques, and project management strategies to ensure successful project implementation.

Existence of competing or unclear expectations will lead your project team to multiple directions, creating disputes that will dismantle trust in your project. Empowering your team in such situations not only resolves the issue but adds to the chaos.

To manage expectations effectively, apply the following principles:

1) Identify all your project stakeholders (internal and external)
2) Study each stakeholder's power, interest, assumed engagement level, and expectations
3) Set expectations with each stakeholder
4) Set the ground rules for engagement/communication, dealing with new/changing expectations, and resolving conflicts
5) Continuously engage with stakeholders
6) Be assertive in dealing with unreasonable expectations

Stakeholder Identification

When I first assumed the role of project manager to implement a project within an education institution, I was initially satisfied with how I managed the project stakeholders. I had built great relationships with the project members, my senior management, project beneficiaries, and the leadership of the client organization. In the first few months everyone was pleased with how smoothly the project progressed.

However, things suddenly changed as the project moved to the first funding milestone. When I submitted the request, as per the agreed process to get funding for the first part of execution to the client organization, my request was returned. I was asked to provide some extensive documentation that I did not know I should have prepared for in the project planning phase. The funding was halted by a mid-level auditor in the client organization who was well-versed in his organization's policies and procedures. I had to work for about two weeks to prepare the requested documentation and resubmit the request for funding. I also had to work with my project sponsor and project team for a longer period to rebuild my trust.

Had I identified the funding auditor as a project's stakeholder and engaged with him directly, I would not have missed the key funding requirement. The organization's leadership did not know exactly how their process worked, so they were not able to provide me with the requirement. I must admit that this was a major blunder in my career, but I did learn my lessons. Putting as much as possible effort to identify all project stakeholders at the beginning of the project is worth it and can save significant cost and effort in the future.

An effective way to identify the project stakeholders is to look for three groups of people, including those who will benefit from, be impacted by, or impact the project (Kloppenborg,

Anantatmula, & Wells, 2015/2019). You can use the business case and project charter as the guiding tool to identify where to look for the project stakeholders. Make sure you involve your project sponsor and project team members throughout the identification process. Devise a tool or a technique that best suits your circumstances and helps you identify your stakeholders efficiently.

Stakeholder Assessment

Once you have identified your project stakeholders, the next key step is to understand how they can impact your project. Engage with the stakeholders directly, where possible, along with your project team to study the project stakeholders' interest, power (over the project), anticipated and desired engagement level, and, most importantly, their expectations from the project. Neglecting to identify one of these key elements in your stakeholders can have a substantial impact on your project and trust within your team, similar to my experience above. Make sure you do not miss the project sponsor (or senior management) and project team as they are vital groups of stakeholders. You cannot establish a shared vision, which is discussed in an earlier chapter, without understanding these two groups in-depth along with other stakeholders.

Expectation Setting

In your stakeholder analysis and information gathering exercise, you may end up building an exhaustive list of expectations. They may not all be realistic and possible for your project to meet them. The major part of your stakeholder evaluation is to examine which expectations your project can meet, and which ones are out of the project's scope. You and your team need to spend a sufficient amount of time to achieve this deliverable. Make sure you engage directly with the relevant stakeholders and provide justifiable explanations for the deliverables that cannot be met. The outcome of this deliverable must be a clear list of agreed-upon expectations by all parties.

Ground Rules

The ground rules should be based on the set of core values (discussed in the previous chapter, *Establish a Shared Vision*) and other guiding principles for communicating and engaging with your stakeholders. The ground rules could also derive from agreements, contracts, Memorandum of Understandings (MOU), or Service Level Agreements (SLA) between your project and its stakeholders. To effectively manage expectations of your stakeholders, make sure the ground rules are set clearly and cover, at the very least, the following areas:

- Communication requirements, tools, methods, and frequencies
- Managing change and dealing with new/changing expectations
- Resolving conflicts

This will help you minimize any potential conflicts that will impact trust between your project and stakeholders.

Continuous Engagement

No matter how explicit expectations are set at the beginning of the project between you and your stakeholders, continuous engagement is still a key determinant of building a trusting relationship with your project stakeholders, thereby maximizing the chance of successful project implementation. When you regularly engage with your project customer and keep them abreast of the project progress, you demonstrate transparency and assure them that the project is in line with their expectations. This will also help you identify and address any discrepancies that might arise along the way.

Engaging with your project sponsor and senior management will ensure your project has their continuous support. Engagement with your own project team, which is a key element of stakeholder management, ensures everyone's expectation is accounted for and the shared vision and high energy remains within the team. Continuous communication with your project partners, suppliers, contractors, and other relevant stakeholders will also ensure reliable collaboration.

Assertiveness

Have you ever seen the type of managers who would say "yes" to every single request from senior management and/or project customer without a rational reasoning as to why? These types of people are those with highly submissive personalities. They just want to keep their bosses happy at that moment and keep their paychecks running. Teams working with such managers feel vulnerable and can never feel empowered. Such managers maximize high uncertainty and distrust within the project environment. Assertive project leaders, on the other hand, make their team members feel empowered and trust their leader (and each other). The team with an assertive leader remains engaged and loyal and makes effective decisions with confidence because they have their leader's back. To be assertive, build on your self-trust and project management and leadership capabilities, and just be a good leader!

***

As the project leader, you should ensure that the expectations set between your project and its stakeholders are realistic and free of any haziness. Keep your stakeholder register up-to-date and continuously engage with project stakeholders to make sure your project is in line with the agreed requirements. Establish an effective measure for managing changes. Finally, play the role of a firewall for any ad hoc and impractical requests that are pushed down to your team from leadership or other stakeholders. This gives your team confidence and commitment to make decisions in the best interests of the project.

Chapter Ten

<u>P</u>romote Creativity

Promoting creativity is about supporting your project team to *move beyond the status-quo* and think outside the box to play their project roles more effectively and efficiently. However, creativity in the project management context is not about gold plating and delivering the product or service with a higher quality than required. It is about constantly looking for the answer to "How can I/we do it better?" By encouraging creative thinking, you give your team the freedom to question existing tools and processes that do not produce valuable results. It helps your team to identify and isolate non-value-added activities from the project while enhancing the actions that add more value to achieving your project objectives.

On personal goals, creativity helps your team to reach their full potentials by trying to put their imagination and dreams into reality. It arouses their passion to work on the project. It improves their confidence and inspires trust in them. An empowered team member with a creative thinking appetite is a great asset for your project.

To promote creativity within your team effectively, apply the following strategies:

1) Set creativity as a core value
2) Recognize and reward team members for *outside the box* thinking
3) Encourage smart risk taking
4) Celebrate mistakes
5) Provide relevant training, resources, and mentorship

Creativity as a Core Value

To maximize creativity in your team, the first step you need to put into motion is to set it as a core value (unless it is against your organizational values in which case you may not be in the right organization anyway!). This will make creative thinking a guiding principle and influence your team's behavior toward it. Focus your team's creativity more on the *how* rather than the *what* aspect of the project. *What* defines the deliverables that need to be accomplished, while *how* is about how to accomplish each of those deliverables to make the product or service. The deliverables are usually the pieces of your product or service and are defined based on agreed upon requirements. Making the deliverables better than agreed will enhance the product or service beyond what is required, called gold-plating as mentioned earlier. When your team instead focuses on the *how* aspect, they come up with better ways of accomplishing the deliverables, therefore saving your project time and effort, and leading to a successful delivery.

Recognition and Reward

There is no value in creativity to be just sitting on a piece of paper as a core value. It must be lived with and demonstrated. An effective way to do this is to establish measures to recognize and reward team members who come up with creative ideas. It does not need to be an official recognition or monetary reward. A simple "thank you" and a mention to the rest of the team goes a long way to intrinsically motivate your team members.

In addition, you can name the individual *Star of the Week* or *Star of the Month*. Make sure when you give credit that it is fair, abundant, and consistent. Giving credit randomly can have a damaging impact on trust and confidence in your team while also giving undeserved compliments that "sound like empty flattery and undermine later efforts that genuinely warrant acknowledgement" (Katzman, 2020, p. 19).

Smart Risk Taking

Creativity comes with both positive and negative risks. When you and your team decide on creative ideas, smart risk taking helps you assess and consider both consequences. In smart risk taking, you get out of your comfort zone; but it does not take you into the threat zone. A new idea might, for instance, have a possibility of fifty percent success with a medium positive impact, while the odds of failure is the same (fifty percent) with a high negative impact. Would you and your team vote to apply this idea to your project? Your decision would depend on your risk appetite levels. Therefore, to ensure smart risk taking, you should establish risk thresholds, provide your team with a risk identification and assessment framework, tools, and resources. Avoid taking any risks without sufficient analysis by relevant subject matter experts.

Celebrating Mistakes

"Anyone who has never made a mistake has never tried anything new" (Einstein, n.d.). While creative ideas can bring great advantages to your project, they are not free of mistakes. Do you remember the famous story about Thomas Edison who tried to create a light bulb more than one thousand times until he succeeded? I am not telling you this to encourage you to try a new idea that many times because your project is constrained with time; but to make the best use of creative behaviors, give your team freedom to make mistakes.

When mistakes happen, work with your relevant team members to analyze what went wrong and how you can do it better in the future. Learning is a great part of making mistakes that helps you and your team to elevate to the next level. According to the prominent neuroscientist, Paul J. Zak, who has performed breakthrough studies on trust from neuroscience perspective, "The best learning is learning through (small) mistakes because such experiences are encoded more powerfully in the brain than when we are simply told a new fact" (Zak, 2017, p. 69). The opposite of celebrating mistakes are mourning mistakes, blaming, and pointing fingers that not only limit creativity but significantly damage the trust and confidence of your team members.

Training, Resources, and Mentorship

To identify or to apply better ways of doing things, and minimize risks of making mistakes, your team may need to receive relevant training and/or resources. Conduct a thorough needs analysis and identify areas where your team members need training and resources. In addition, keep your door open to your team so they can comfortably come to you with their needs and requests. Make sure you provide equal and fair opportunities to all your team members. A minor disparity could have dire consequences of a lack of trust within your project.

Some of your team members may have great potential that could be complimented with your continuous support and mentorship.

Identify these individuals and establish an effective approach to mentor them. This goes a long way to building your credibility and a strong relationship with your team.

***

Empowered team members who have the freedom to be creative become engaged and passionate in what they do. This builds on their self-confidence and trust in the team. To encourage creative thinking, make it a priority, reward, and recognize your team for coming with new ideas; establish an effective risk assessment framework to minimize negative risks of creativity, leave room for mistakes, and, finally, provide needed resources, training, and continuous support to each team member.

Chapter Eleven

<u>O</u>ptimize Stakeholder Collaboration

Collaboration means that your stakeholders, including your project team, senior management, customer, end-users, partners, suppliers, and contractors, work together to achieve the project goals and create the desired benefits. Collaboration and trust are closely interrelated. You collaborate with those whom you trust, and you trust those whom you collaborate with. In other words, collaboration and trust reinforce each other. In addition, collaboration from one side inspires trust and stimulates reciprocal collaboration from the other side. I have always observed effective collaboration to be a key determinant of successful project delivery.

When your project stakeholders collaborate, they inspire trust in each other, thereby leading to transparent communication and exchange of information throughout the project lifecycle. This will help you measure project progress more accurately and give you a better visibility over potential project issues and risks, therefore ensuring detection and prevention of problems and defects in a timely manner.

To optimize stakeholder collaboration, apply the following principles:

1) Set collaboration as a core value

2) Create a win-win mindset in your project environment

3) Address the "elephant in the room"

4) Place the right person in the right role

5) Share success, own failures

6) Enable a 360-degree feedback loop

7) Incorporate effective team building activities

Collaboration as a Core Value

First and foremost, to optimize collaboration in your project environment, you should work with your team and organization to make it a core value for the project. Define what collaboration means and how your team envisions to achieve it. Also, identify success criteria and metrics to help you measure your team's performance based on collaborative behavior of its members. To prioritize this behavior, an optimal approach would be to make it a key performance indicator (KPI) in your team's performance plan. However, collaboration as a KPI can only be limited to the team you or your organization directly manages.

In that case, demonstrating collaboration as a core value in your behavior inspires a reciprocal reaction in your stakeholders. Where possible, in your project agreements with partners, set collaboration as an essential expected behavior and success criterion.

Win-win Mindset

As noted earlier, collaboration is about working together as a team to achieve a common goal. A key prerequisite to optimizing collaboration in your project is having a win-win mindset across your project. Win-win thinking is present when your stakeholders believe that if the project succeeds, everyone will succeed; and if the project loses, everyone will lose.

A win-win attitude is manifested in a survival group game; for instance, in which group members will have to work together to survive (e.g., a shared goal). To win the game, the players must establish clear expectations from each other, identify a winning strategy, assign roles and responsibilities, and finally abide by the game rules. If one player misses a step, the whole group could lose.

A win-win mindset is established in the same manner in a project. First, the project leader should work with the team to assess and understand the expectations of all project stakeholders. Second, based on expectations, the team should create a shared picture among all the project's stakeholders about the end-goal of the project. Then they should define and assign tasks, roles, and responsibilities to each stakeholder. Finally, the team should establish ground rules to determine success criteria for effective collaboration and to deal with any discrepancies. If any of the key foundations discussed here is lacking in a project, it could hinder the creation of a win-win mindset, resulting in a low collaborative project environment.

Elephant in the Room

Elephant in the room (not to be mistaken with *white elephant in the room,* which means an idea or solution that initially seemed attractive but is not attractive anymore*)* is a common metaphorical expression that refers to "an obvious major problem or issue that people avoid discussing or acknowledging" (Merriam-Webster, 2020).

When there is a controversial topic that your stakeholders intentionally avoid discussing, that is, in fact, a sign of ongoing conflict that could have a negative impact on your team members' collaborative behavior, besides undermining their trust, confidence, and commitment. A minor controversial issue could turn to a major problem if it remains unresolved for long time. In addition, it demonstrates your and your organization's weakness, and makes you less reliable when you do not address such unresolved topics.

To address the elephant in the room, first acknowledge that one exists. Next, work with your relevant stakeholders to identify and apply the best solution. Your leadership, conflict resolution, objectivity, intercultural, and emotional intelligence competencies are key to addressing the elephant in the room effectively.

Right Person in the Right Role

A highly collaborative environment exists when its team is created of good *mix and match* members. This happens when you put the right people in the right roles. The right person is the one whose behaviors and competencies are in line with your project culture and values. A candidate who believes that working solo is the best approach to work will not be a good match (regardless of their other competencies) when collaboration is a priority for your project. If hired, this single individual could build a big elephant in the room, poisoning your whole project environment.

Next, you must ensure that the person you select is placed in the right role. This happens when the candidate's skills, capabilities, and interests match the role that they will be playing in the project. Mismatch in role distribution causes low motivation, therefore leading to a lack of purpose for collaboration.

To put the right person in the right role, first identify the behaviors and competencies that your project requires. Second, define the specific skills and capabilities that you require each role player to possess and include the requisite specifications in the job description. Next, design your interview questions in a way that helps you identify those characteristics. The interview does not have to be a structured one. An unstructured interview might give you a better opportunity to find the right people for your project. Finally, conduct the interview by making your interviewee feel comfortable so they can speak from their heart. This happens when you speak from your heart!

Success and Failure

Your leadership approach is vital in developing a culture of collaboration within your team. One of the traits you should build on is your behavior toward project successes and failures. If success ultimately goes to you and failure is pointed toward the team, your team members will not only be unwilling to cooperate, but there will also be a feeling of distrust, hesitation, and low morale across your project environment. In such cases, conspiracy theories and negative politics will be used as primary tools by some members and groups to survive allegations. When the project leader, on the other hand, gives credit to his team for project accomplishments and takes responsibility of project issues and failures, the same behavior cascades down to the project team which will result in a high sense of accountability, transparency, and trust across the project.

Owning failures does not, however, imply that you should ignore the team and individual performance issues that cause those failures. First, as the project leader, you must proactively work with your team to identify and address any potential performance issues. You can do this by continuously assessing your team's needs and providing relevant training, resources, mentorship, and support. If a defect or failure occurs due to performance issues, identify the root cause and the individuals who were involved, but do not publicize who they are. You should own the failure in the eye of others (as you are ultimately accountable for the project) while working individually with the concerned individuals to address the issue. This will give your team members a great sense of accountability and motivation to rectify and avoid similar problems in the future.

360-degree Feedback

As evident by its name, 360-degree feedback (which originated in the military more than one-hundred years ago and introduced into the business industry in the 1950s), is used to gather behavior and performance feedback on a team member from all levels, including the team member themselves, their managers, peers, customers, and direct reports (Organisation Development

& Research Limited, 2020). If done appropriately, this is a great approach to boost collaboration across the project. It also maximizes your objectivity to identify strengths and areas of improvement in your team members. Make 360-degree feedback part of your performance management and development framework. The key to successful 360-degree feedback implementation is the way you structure your questions which ensures that the respondents provide constructive feedback.

Team Building Activities

Team building activities are crucial in building mutual understanding, trust, and ultimately strong relationships among your stakeholders. All these elements can maximize collaboration in your project. Make sure you plan and incorporate effective team building activities. Your regular team meetings are a good place to integrate some team building games and activities. You can also plan some of your events offline (like in a bowling alley or golf club, depending on your budget and your team's interest) to celebrate certain milestones while building relationships with your team.

***

Collaboration is the engine of building a trustful project environment. Empowered team members make effective decisions when other team members and stakeholders cooperate with them. To optimize collaboration in your project, prioritize it by setting it as a guiding principle, build a win-win way of thinking, acknowledge and address unspoken controversial topics, hire the right people and place them in the right roles, give credit for success and take responsibility for failures, apply 360-degree feedback framework, and implement effective team building activities.

Chapter Twelve

<u>W</u>alk the Talk

I have a daughter, Armaghan. As of writing this book, she is eight years old. Bragging aside, she is great at following instructions. When she was about five, she came to me with her iPad on the dinner table. I kindly explained to her that it was not good manners to use electronics on the dining table. We both agreed that going forward it would be part of our rules not to use electronics on the dining table. She followed the rule for a long time until one day I saw her with the iPad again. I got upset and reminded her of the rule. She said "Dad, is this rule only for me? [The other day] I saw you talking to your friend on your phone while you were eating dinner." Yes, she was right. I felt embarrassed and accepted my mistake. I asked her and my wife to choose a punishment and I was timed out for an hour in my bedroom. Since then, I carefully match my words with my actions in the family so I do not fail in *walking my talk*.

My story should remind you of the common expression, *actions speak louder than words.* The same holds true in building trust with your project stakeholders. Stakeholders do not look at your words; they look at your actions, and that is how they rely on you. No matter how great your vision looks, how precious your core values are, or how beautiful your words sound, if you do not do what you say, they mean nothing to your team. It is what you do that sets the tone for everything that you envision your team to pursue.

To walk the talk effectively, apply the following principles:

1) Be the role model
2) Do not make unrealistic commitments
3) Write down your actions and commitments, and follow through with them
4) Let your team hold you accountable
5) Admit your mistakes
6) Be consistent

The Role Model

My daughter's story is a good example that demonstrates the importance of being the role model as a leader. The best way to convey what the core values of your organization or project are is to live them. The beautiful value statements on your billboards can only do a little to influence your team's behaviors if your actions do not represent those values.

I once worked in an organization where *collaboration (within and across teams)* was stated as one of their five core values. The first executive lead of our workstream was a great role model for collaboration. When it came to cooperation and working together, he did not have a line to show his team versus other teams. He had an open-door policy and collaborated equally with everyone across the organization. He inspired not only our group as his team but everyone he worked with. Cross-functional working groups were naturally formed to work on our workstream deliverables. Coordination was fun until he moved on and we had our next leader.

The new leader's behavior indicated that he liked working in silos and only focused on his team. It was not that long until everyone's cooperative behavior declined to match the new leader's approach. Cooperation became a challenge even within the team and accomplishing tasks and deliverables started taking more time than they did before.

This experience taught me a great lesson about the significance of leaders setting the example. Followers can quickly adapt their behaviors to match those of their leaders. To remain as a role model, constantly assess your behaviors against your organization's values and make sure they are in line. It may be easier said than done but it is the only way to set your team's standards because "so goes the leader, so goes the culture" (Sinek, 2014 & 2017, p. 171).

Unrealistic Commitments

Making hasty and unrealistic commitments is a serious trap to your credibility. If you promise something that you cannot fulfill, that creates a significant discrepancy between your *talk* and *walk*, leading to a feeling of distrust by your team. Make sure you devote sufficient time to evaluate the feasibility of your commitments before you make them.

Writing Down Actions

As a project leader, you may have a lot on your plate that could go beyond your memory capacity. In other words, your memory may be full or even overused (God forbid!) where you have no space to save and remember a verbal promise you have made. This challenge could lead you to inadvertently fail on fulfilling your promises. Therefore, writing down your actions and commitments is important to avoid the risk of failing to deliver on your promises.

Writing the tasks down in one place is an important step toward making them easier to track. Besides physical notepads, there are a wide range of notepad computer applications (both built-in and add-ons) that you could choose from. However, do not get swamped with all these options. Just pick one that best meets your needs and stick with it.

Others Holding You Accountable

If you want to hold your team members accountable, allow them to hold you accountable as well. Let them question you for the mistakes you have made and the promises you have missed. This is a vital attribute of leaders who work to maximize transparency, fairness, and accountability within their teams. This is closely linked to our discussion about being the role model. It is your actions that inspire similar actions and set the path for your team to follow.

Admitting a Mistake

Admitting your mistakes is not easy. It may come with feelings of embarrassment, shame, or guilt, but it is an extremely potent way to hold yourself accountable and build trust with your team. In addition, admitting your mistakes sets an example for others to follow and helps to avoid many problems that could be caused by the missteps of you or your team. Once you realize that you have made a mistake, acknowledge it as soon as possible to minimize the ripple effect. Also, make sure you identify and propose the resolution, and communicate the lessons you have learned from your blunders.

Being Consistent

Consistency is extremely important to your credibility and reputation. Randomly walking the talk has adverse effects in your project environment. It creates uncertainties and maximizes feelings of hesitation and doubt within your project. Think of the top brand products and services in any industry. What is common about them? I believe it is delivering quality products and services *consistently*. It is consistent effective behaviors and actions that build one's reputation and reliability.

* * *

To establish your credibility and set an example for your team, always strive to do what you promise and believe in. Encourage and act on constructive criticism and let your team question your decisions. Do not make unfeasible promises and record the ones that you make so you can track and act on them. If you make a mistake, learn from it, and admit it as soon as you notice it. Finally, show a consistent behavior.

Chapter Thirteen

<u>E</u>licit Feedback

Feedback is your food to remain focused, efficient, and effective. When you regularly ask for feedback from your stakeholders, you open yourself up to criticism, establish a culture of openness and accountability, and create an opportunity to identify and tighten loose ends. Loose ends in your project could have a detrimental impact on trust and your team's confidence to make effective decisions.

In addition, seeking feedback, if done appropriately, helps you identify and amend strategies, behaviors, and processes that do not work effectively. In other words, you let your team and stakeholders, who may have better visibility, detect nonvalue-added activities, which, ultimately, will increase their sense of accountability, trust, and confidence. Seeking feedback, therefore, functions as a particularly useful way to build a trustful project environment.

To elicit feedback effectively, apply the following principles:

1) Use both structured and unstructured feedback gathering methods
2) Involve all stakeholders

3) Ask the right questions

4) Listen empathically

5) Keep your door open 24/7

6) Act on feedback

Feedback Methods

You can solicit feedback both in a structured and an unstructured manner. In a structured feedback gathering approach, questions are identified in advance; for example, in the form of a survey. You can focus the survey on a specific area or make it general. It could, for example, be about how your team views either your approach toward stakeholder management or your project management and leadership style in general.

Unstructured feedback gathering can sometimes be a much better way to identify opportunities for improvement and build a trustful relationship. As obvious by its name, this type of feedback solicitation is ad hoc and informal. You ask for feedback on your performance when you feel you need to. You can also establish a process and tool that your stakeholder uses to send you feedback when they want to. Either way, it makes your stakeholders feel important and heard, leading you to having a strong rapport with them.

Involving all Stakeholders

While you may be interacting more closely with your project team, treat your stakeholders equally across the project when it comes to asking for feedback. If you solicit feedback from one group and leave out the other, you inadvertently demonstrate that the other group is less important to you. This creates an environment of negative politics and can undermine trust and confidence in your project.

Asking the Right Questions

When you ask for feedback using either a structured or unstructured approach, make sure you devise questions in a manner that helps you gather useful advice from your stakeholders. Asking open-ended questions rather than predefined multiple-choice answers or questions with yes/no answers is a better way to let your stakeholders speak their minds. By using multiple-choice answers, you may convey a wrong message that you are only interested to hear the answers that you want, while the yes/no questioning format (close-ended) limits their ability to provide comprehensive feedback.

Asking questions in the right way and at the right moment are also important. When you ask for feedback in person, be friendly and authentic. Show that you are really interested in their suggestions. However, depending on the situation, you may not hear your favorite words or the way you expect to hear them. Set the example by keeping empathic, professional, and calm, and let others follow.

In terms of structured feedback through surveys, although the need for anonymity may be a sign that you need more work to build on trust and transparency in your project, if you believe that making surveys anonymous can help you gather more open and realistic feedback, do so. Allowing your team to share their opinions with you openly is a key step to building trust.

Listening Empathically

As the project lead, you can get extremely busy and your mind may be in a thousand places at one time. With some people, this challenge can build an unwanted skill of *listening in the autopilot mode*. Avoid this habit at any cost. This is dangerous for you as a project leader. When you are caught in the autopilot listening mode, your credibility as an empathic leader could be undermined and you might need to work for a long time to recover the trust you had.

To listen emphatically, avoid any distractions, focus your mind and full attention to that very moment of conversation with your stakeholder, listen with your ears (to the words and tone) and eyes (to the body language), repeat phrases to confirm understanding, and ask clarifying questions. Refrain from any gestures that could misrepresent your intentions. Also, make sure you help conclude the conversation with any relevant follow up actions. Write down all action items on your notepad to make sure you do not forget what you promised.

Being Available 24/7

Sometimes your stakeholders might have a concern that is time sensitive and could escalate if not shared in an urgent manner. For example, let's say you have a monthly progress meeting with your project client first thing tomorrow morning. One of your team members suddenly finds out that evening that your calculations for Deliverable A Percentage Complete is not accurate. If you have already established a 24/7 open door policy, your team member will share with you their concerns in time without any hesitation, thereby ensuring that accurate information is communicated to the client. Having your door open at all times is crucial in avoiding minor concerns turning into major problems.

Acting on Feedback

Acting on feedback you receive is vital to retaining your open-door policy and encouraging your stakeholders to provide you with useful suggestions. During any feedback session, make sure you draw and agree on relevant actions. Write them down and follow up on each action. Not doing so will not only minimize valuable ideas by your stakeholders in the future, but will also make them reluctant to listen to and act on your feedback. This will eventually impact trust on both sides.

***

To build a trustful and empowered atmosphere in your project, do not only be open to feedback, but proactively engage with your stakeholders to provide you with their opinions about you and your project management and leadership. Base your feedback gathering format on your circumstances and project culture. To establish an effective feedback culture, involve all stakeholders, ask relevant questions, listen with empathy, be open to suggestions, and act on any suggestions and concerns that are shared with you.

Chapter Fourteen
<u>R</u>eadjust as Needed

Rigid project management and leadership pose a major risk to trust and confidence levels of a team. In addition, rigidity can make your team focus on obsolete tools and processes (established earlier in the project) that do not add any value to your project anymore, thereby lowering the team's motivation and morale.

As noted earlier in this book, change is inevitable given the fast-paced environment experienced in the workplace today. To effectively remain on target, your approach should be resilient and flexible enough to maximize continuous improvement and account for changing circumstances. You should proactively work with your project stakeholders to identify gaps and areas of improvement, and readjust as needed.

To effectively readjust, apply the following strategies:

1) Set continuous improvement as a core value
2) Adopt agility
3) Identify lessons learned consistently
4) Plan and apply readjustments
5) Assess changes for effectiveness

Continuous Improvement as a Core Value

A key step to a successful readjustment strategy is to make continuous improvement a core value of your project. Work with your team to define what continuous improvement means for your project and how you will achieve it.

However, be sure to draw a clear line between gold-plating and the continuous improvement mindset. Your team's goal should not be to improve the product or service more than what your project customer asked for and you agreed on. Rather, it should be focused on improving the processes to minimize waste and maximize successful delivery of the product or service within budget, on time, on scope, and on quality. Continuous improvement mindset also triggers the creative thinking we discussed in Chapter 10.

Adopting Agility

Agility is an extremely important quality in continuous improvement. If you or your team identifies an area of improvement but takes a long time to act upon it, your efforts will be wasted. Identify and detach rigid processes that hinders or decelerates your agility. Wherever possible in your project, integrate agile practices to facilitate identification of areas of improvement, potential risks, issues, and to help implement corrective actions.

Identifying Lessons Learned Consistently

Lessons learned identification is usually known to be one of the last project activities in the closing phase. Its aim is to reflect on experiences gained from the project and find out answers, at the very least, to the following questions:

- What went well during the project? What did not go as expected? What could be done differently?
- What should we continue doing in similar projects in the future? What should we stop doing? What should we start doing?

However, similar questions (with slight changes as noted below) should be asked constantly by each project team member to identify lessons learned and improve processes in the current project.

- What did I/we do well to complete task X? What did not go as I/we expected? What could I/we do differently?
- What should I/we continue doing to complete similar tasks in the future? What should I/we stop doing? What should I/we start doing?

Identifying lessons learned should be integrated as part of continuous process improvement. This will ensure the project benefits persistently from experiences being gained by the project team.

Applying Readjustments

Once you've identified areas of improvement and corrective actions, the next step is to work with your project team and stakeholders to plan and implement the relevant changes. The change, however, may directly relate to you and not necessarily be associated with the rest of the project. For example, based on your own reflections or your team's feedback, you may decide to alter your project management or leadership approach. In either case, you will need to make sure you have a thorough plan in place to implement the relevant readjustments. Be sure to have a rollback plan in place to undo the change in case things fail to go as expected.

Assessment

Assessment is a very important part of a successful readjustment. Once you have implemented the change, your next key deliverable is to monitor the change closely to make sure it has been implemented as you planned, and it is creating the benefits or making the impact that you or your team

107

intended. If you find out that the change generates adverse effects, then it is time to implement your rollback plan. Keep evaluating the change until you or your team is confident that it has been successful.

***

When your team understands that they are not locked into rigid policies, procedures, and/or processes, they will feel empowered and confident. They will trust you for creating a culture of effective resilience and agility by promoting continuous improvement and adopting best practices to identify, plan, and integrate improvements.

Chapter Fifteen

All in One Place

Trust is the backbone of every project that runs from project inception to closing, both vertically and horizontally. Completing a project successfully without the factor of trust is only a myth. Why is trust so vital in project management? To mention just a few benefits, trust helps to ensure:

- Projects plan realistically by creating an environment of openness and accountability
- The project is executed successfully through keeping the team motivated, interested, committed, and transparent
- Monitoring and controlling are not only done at the project and/or team level, but also at the individual level which helps improve performance, improve quality, and prevent problems
- The project's final product (or service) is delivered successfully to the client through trusting stakeholder relationships
- Project agility and continuous customer engagement is maintained throughout the project by creating a win-win mindset and creating a transparent environment for interactions

The Final EMPOWER Framework to Build Trust

The following table aggregates our discussion and provides you with a comprehensive framework to build trust in projects using my proposed EMPOWER strategy. Use this framework as a tool and reference to identify your strengths and areas of needed focus to leverage and ensure a trusting relationship with your project stakeholders.

Figure 15.1: EMPOWER Framework to Build Trust

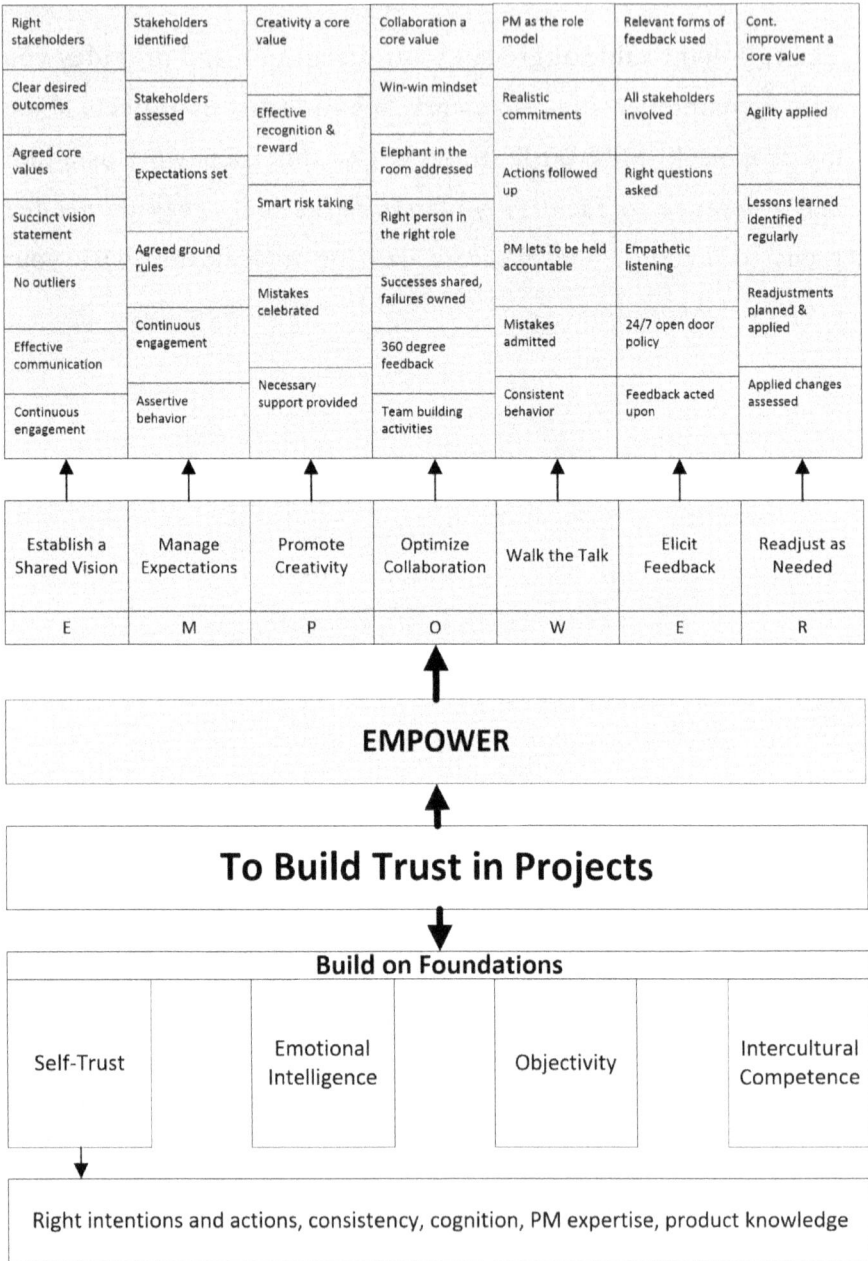

Right stakeholders	Stakeholders identified	Creativity a core value	Collaboration a core value	PM as the role model	Relevant forms of feedback used	Cont. improvement a core value
Clear desired outcomes	Stakeholders assessed	Effective recognition & reward	Win-win mindset	Realistic commitments	All stakeholders involved	Agility applied
Agreed core values	Expectations set		Elephant in the room addressed	Actions followed up	Right questions asked	
Succinct vision statement	Agreed ground rules	Smart risk taking	Right person in the right role	PM lets to be held accountable	Empathetic listening	Lessons learned identified regularly
No outliers	Continuous engagement	Mistakes celebrated	Successes shared, failures owned	Mistakes admitted	24/7 open door policy	Readjustments planned & applied
Effective communication			360 degree feedback			
Continuous engagement	Assertive behavior	Necessary support provided	Team building activities	Consistent behavior	Feedback acted upon	Applied changes assessed

Establish a Shared Vision	Manage Expectations	Promote Creativity	Optimize Collaboration	Walk the Talk	Elicit Feedback	Readjust as Needed
E	M	P	O	W	E	R

EMPOWER

To Build Trust in Projects

Build on Foundations

Self-Trust	Emotional Intelligence	Objectivity	Intercultural Competence

Right intentions and actions, consistency, cognition, PM expertise, product knowledge

I hope this reading has been worthy of your time and focus. I am very much looking forward to having your reflection and feedback. Thank you and best wishes!

jamshed.adel@pm-panacea.com

https://pm-panacea.com/contact-us

References

Anderson, L. W., & Krathwohl, D. R. (n.d.). *A taxonomy for learning, teaching, and assessing: a revision of Bloom's taxonomy of education objectives/editors, Lorin W. Anderson, David Krathwohl; contributors, Peter W. Airasian et al. (Complete ed.).* Longman.

Beck, K., Beedle, M., Bennekum, A. v., Cockburn, A., Cunningham, W., Fowler, M., . . . Thomas, D. (2001). *Manifesto for Agile Software Development.* Retrieved from agilemanifesto.org: http://agilemanifesto.org/iso/en/manifesto.html

Bodhi, B. (1984, 1994). *The Noble Eightfold Path: The Way to the End of Suffering.* Onalaska: Pariyatti Publishing.

Bracey, H. (2010). *Building Trust: How to Get It! How to Keep It!* Hyler Bracey.

Bradberry, T., & Greaves, J. (2009). *Emotional Intelligence 2.0.* San Diego: TalentSmart.

Cobb, G. C. (2015). *The Project Manager's Guide to Mastering Agile: Principles and Practices for an Adaptive Approach.* New Jersey: John Wiley & Sons, Inc.

Covey, S. M., & Merrill, R. R. (2018). *The Speed of Trust: The One Thing That Changes Everything.* New York: Free Press.

Cultural Detective. (n.d.). *Why Intercultural Competence?* Retrieved from culturaldetective.com: https://www.culturaldetective.com/why/intercultural-competence.html

Einstein, A. (n.d.). *Brainy Quote*. Retrieved from
   BraintyQuote.com:
   https://www.brainyquote.com/quotes/albert_einstein_10
   9012#

Feltman, C. (2009). *The Thin Book of Trust: An Essential
   Primer for Building Trust at Work*. Bend: Think Book
   Publishing Co.

Franklin, B. (n.d.). *Brainy Quote*. Retrieved from
   BraintyQuote.com:
   https://www.brainyquote.com/quotes/benjamin_franklin
   _138217

Goleman, D. (1995, 2005). *Emotional Intelligence: Why It Can
   Matter More Than IQ*. New York: Bantam Dell.

Hemingway, E. (n.d.). *Brainy Quote*. Retrieved from
   BrainyQuote.com:
   https://www.brainyquote.com/quotes/ernest_hemingway
   _383691

Imudia, M. I., Kaindaneh, P. M., & Baffour-Awuah, D. (2013).
   Why Projects FAIL in the Public Sector. Middletown,
   DE: Siotoh, LLC.

Katzman, M. A. (2020). *Connect First: 52 Simple Ways to
   Ignite Success, Meaning, and Joy at Work*. McGraw
   Hill.

Kloppenborg, T. J., Anantatmula, V., & Wells, K. N.
   (2015/2019). *Contemporary Project Management,
   Fourth Edition*. Boston: Cengage Learning.

Kouzes, J. M., & Posner, B. (2009). *To Lead, Create a Shared
   Vision*. Retrieved from Harvard Business Review:
   https://hbr.org/2009/01/to-lead-create-a-shared-vision

Malone, T. (2009). *Infoenza: Why Projects Fail and How to
   Fix Them*.

McChrystal, S. (2011, April 6). *Listen, learn...then lead.* Retrieved from Youtube.Com. TED Conferences: https://www.youtube.com/watch?v=FmpIMt95ndU

Merriam-Webster. (2020, June 14). Retrieved from Merriam-Webster.com: https://www.merriam-webster.com/dictionary/trust

Merriam-Webster. (2020, July 27). Retrieved from Merriam-Webster.com: https://www.merriam-webster.com/dictionary/elephant%20in%20the%20room

Mwanza, G. C., & Namusokwe, M. (2015). *Why Projects Fail.* Wandsbeck, South Africa.

Oldfield, N. D. (2017). *The Power of Trust: How Top Companies Build, Manage and Protect It.* Canada: Natalie C. Doyle Oldfield.

Organisation Development & Research Limited. (2020, July 28). *Organisation Development & Research Limited.* Retrieved from www.odrl.org: https://www.odrl.org/2019/12/27/360-degree-feedback-history/

Project Management Institute. (2017). *A Guide to the Project Management Body of Knowledge: PMBOK® Guide.* Project Management Institute.

Schwartz, S. G. (2018). *Creating a Greater Whole: A Project Manager's Guide to Becoming a Leader.* Boca Raton: CRC Press, Taylor & Francis Group.

Shauchenka, U. (2013). *Why Projects Fail.*

Sinek, S. (2014, 2017). *Leaders Eat Last: Why Some Teams Pull Together and Others Don't.* New York: Portfolio Penguin. p. 171.

Sinek, S. (2014, 2017). *Leaders Eat Last: Why Some Teams Pull Together and Others Don't.* New York: Portfolio Penguin. p. 279.

Stepanek, G. (2005). *Software Project Secrets: Why Software Projects Fail.* New York: Apress.

The Standish Group International, Inc. (2015). *Chaos Report 2015.* The Standish Group International, Inc.

Thornton, D. M. (2008). *Trust or Bust! How to Win By Building Trust in the Workplace.* Trafford Publishing.

U.S. Department of Transportation. (2001). *Engineering Analysis Report and Initial Decision Regarding EA00-23: Firestone Wilderness AT Tires.* National Highway Traffic Safety Administration, Office of Defects Investigation. U.S. Department of Transportation.

Vanderbilt University Center for Teaching. (n.d.). *Center for Teaching.* Retrieved from Vanderbilt: https://cft.vanderbilt.edu/guides-sub-pages/blooms-taxonomy/

Zak, P. J. (2017). *Trust Factor: The Science of Creating High Performance Companies.* New York: AMACOM. p. 69

Zak, P. J. (2017). *Trust Factor: The Science of Creating High-Performance Companies.* New York: AMACOM.

About the Author

A. Jamshed Adel is the founder of PM-Panacea, a project management consulting and training firm. He is a certified Project Management Professional (PMP®) and Project Management Institute Risk Management Professional (PMI-RMP®) with over a decade of experience in project management that involves managing and leading large and complex projects. He holds a master's degree in project management from Georgetown University. As a passionate consultant, Jamshed's goal is to explore and surface some of the vital principles of project management and help organizations and project managers choose the right methods, tools and techniques thereby maximizing successful delivery of projects.

www.ingramcontent.com/pod-product-compliance
Lightning Source LLC
Chambersburg PA
CBHW071900020426
42331CB00010B/2609